The Royal Touch

SIMPLY STUNNING HOME COOKING
FROM A FORMER ROYAL CHEF

Carolyn Robb

ACC ART BOOKS

To Mum
My inspiration and the greatest cook of all

First published in 2015 by ACC Editions
Reprinted 2017
Published in 2019 by ACC Art Books
Reprinted 2020

ISBN: 978-1-78884-045-3

British Library Cataloguing-in-Publication Data
A catalogue record for this book is available from the British Library

Printed in China by ACC Art Books Ltd., Woodbridge, Suffolk, UK
www.accartbooks.com

**ACC
ART
BOOKS**

Contents

Acknowledgements

Many hugely talented people have poured their energy, creativity and enthusiasm into this book; I am indebted to all of you. Others have afforded me the incredible opportunities and extraordinary experiences that have enabled and inspired me to put pen to paper; for which no thank you is big enough. I could never have done this without all those who have unceasingly encouraged and supported me in my endeavours; not just during the writing of this book but for many years.

Mum & Dad

Your unconditional love, your immense generosity, your wisdom, your wonderful guidance and your infectious enthusiasm made you the best parents anyone could wish for. You worked so incredibly hard and gave me so much; in particular, the confidence to follow my dreams. How I wish there had been a way to say a big enough 'THANK YOU' to you both. Mum, you

were the finest cookery teacher in the world; and with your amazing spirit and enormous optimism nothing ever seemed insurmountable. Dad, your appreciation of some of the burnt offerings that I put before you as an experimenting 6-year-old chef, made me believe that I could cook long before I really could cook at all. It was that belief, which spurred me on to much greater things.

Your Royal Highness

(THE PRINCE OF WALES)

Thank you for eleven incredible, inspirational and exciting years as YRH's chef. It was quite simply my dream job. As a very young chef cooking for YRH, I was afforded a lifetime's worth of extraordinarily special experiences and opportunities. I learnt so much that I still carry with me. I feel immensely privileged to have cooked for such a wonderful family.

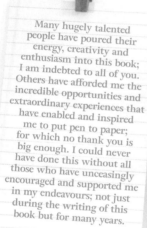

James Smith

OF ACC ART BOOKS

Thank you for believing in my book and for producing this long-awaited English version. I cannot wait to hold the first copy in my hands!

Susannah Hecht

OF ACC ART BOOKS

Thank you so much for your huge contribution to this book. Your attention to detail is astonishing. (I apologise for all the mis-placed and missing commas... I promise to get them all in the right places next time!)

Bill Schwartz

Thank you for your energetic support over the past few years and during the process of bringing all aspects of this book together. As well as reaching an agreement with the best possible publisher for my book, you also secured the wonderful creative talents that have transformed my vision for this special book into a reality. Your enthusiasm, diligence and hard work are greatly appreciated.

Beth Price

A very big thank you for so thoroughly dissecting each recipe as you tested it. You left no detail to chance and I feel reassured that these recipes will now work equally well on both sides of the Atlantic Ocean.

Sarah Champier

To my good friend and florist extraordinaire, a heartfelt thank you for the flowers that appear in the book, they are beautiful.

Acknowledgements

Your Royal Highnesses

(THE DUKE AND DUCHESS OF GLOUCESTER)

A huge thank you for welcoming me so warmly into your household when, fresh from cookery school, I still had so much to learn. It could not have been a more perfect first job, nor a happier two years, and there was not a day when I didn't look forward to putting on my apron in the morning. I carry with me such happy memories of that time.

Deirdre Reford

My wonderful sister, the very biggest thank you of all goes to you. Without your support I would not even have contemplated embarking on this huge project. You have done everything imaginable to help me. For all the baby-sitting, proof-reading, editing, recipe testing, dog walking, moral support, sound advice and encouragement at all times of day and night, there really is no thank you that comes anywhere near to being adequate!

Rachel Bonness

The design and layout of this book is sensational (or should I say 'Simply Stunning'!) Thank you so much. Not only have you demonstrated huge talent and flair but also great patience in dealing with the many last minute requests and my never-ending lists of amendments… You have shown amazing efficiency in working to such short deadlines.

Simon Brown

Thank you for the beautiful photographs; your work is amazing. The shoot days were long but being greeted on arrival with one of your hand-crafted cups of coffee, always made all the difference! **LIZ BAUENS** thank you for taking such trouble to source and select such great props and for letting me take over your kitchen.

Katy Aldrich, Sally Reford, Rebecca Varian, Tessa Vardigans & Sheena Wooding

Thank you to each one of you for giving up a day to come with me to one of the many photo shoots to help with looking after Mandy. Your expert baby-sitting made all the difference to us both – we could not have managed without you!

Lucy & Mandy

My beautiful girls, Big Hugs and a huge THANK YOU for being such an inspiration to me. You've been so patient during the many long hours I've spent cooking and writing. Lucy, almost every night you've asked, "Is that book finished yet Mummy?" I'm so happy that at last I can say "Yes"! Mandy, you came to every photo shoot, and at just 4 months old you smiled your way through endless hours in the front pack while we deliberated over dustings of icing sugar and scatterings of herbs. Thank you for being so good natured.

Rodney Robb, Stuart Robb & John Robb

Thank you to the best big brothers in the world. Despite being scattered so far and wide, you are always there to help, each in your own special way with anything and everything I do.

Akane Nakano

Thank you for your stunning illustrations; so perfect in every detail. I'm sure you must have worked through the night many times to get them all done. From the small and simple ones – an apple, a bowl of sugar, a sack of flour – to the intricate and complex palaces and castles; they really deserve a whole book to themselves!

Introduction
BY CAROLYN ROBB

This collection of a hundred of my best-loved recipes represents so many happy memories from the fascinating 'culinary journey' that I have travelled. It is a journey that has covered three continents over several decades and has taken in many a royal palace along the way. The highlight has been the extraordinarily special people that I have been so privileged to encounter; both in and out of the kitchen.

I have drawn inspiration for my recipes from far and wide, however, my food remains simple and homely. I grew up in South Africa, where from no age at all I was at my mother's side in the kitchen. She was a wonderful cook, a great teacher to me and her recipes never seemed to fail! She gave me a brilliant foundation in cookery skills. Later, my Cordon Bleu diploma acted as a great springboard from which I bounded joyously into my first job, as chef to TRH The Duke and Duchess of Gloucester at Kensington Palace. Two years after that I moved just a hundred yards up the road, still within the palace, when I became chef to TRH The Prince and Princess of Wales and the young Princes William and Harry. My thirteen years in the royal household were filled with incredible experiences and I have so many happy memories of this time.

Kensington Palace

I subsequently lived and worked in Dubai and California, both of which gave me fascinating insights into new and very different cuisines, cultures and lifestyles. I came away with many fresh ideas and new perspectives on food. Now I have two beautiful little girls to cook for and nothing makes me happier than to see them enjoying their meals. I treasure the time that I spend teaching them simple skills in the kitchen – it's never too early to start learning to love cooking and to appreciate good food!

In the *Little Bites* chapter, you will find simple recipes for children. As far as possible I cook with organic ingredients for my girls, and I know that many parents strive to do the same for their children, even when they cannot stretch to eating organic food themselves. It is not always readily available and it can be expensive, which is why I suggest organic ingredients 'if you can' in each recipe.

Lucy and Mandy

I tested all the recipes for this book in the tiny kitchen in my 350 year-old cottage. It is a cosy, homely space with low ceilings and exposed beams; it is the simplest of kitchens! I also prepared all the food for the pictures in this book at home. There are no catches in the recipes and there is nothing tricky about them. They can be prepared just about anywhere and by anyone. Within recipes I frequently suggest variations and alternatives and I urge you to make substitutions of ingredients with confidence and conviction (being guided by what is in season or what is growing in your garden or on your allotment).

The recipes have also been tested in America, and we know that they all work perfectly there too. Measures have been converted to imperial weights and American volumetric units, rounded up or down from UK metric measurements. (1 cup = 250ml, 1 Tablespoon = 15ml and 1 teaspoon = 5ml). It is always important to measure carefully. Where cooking terminology and the names of ingredients differ, everything is referenced in detail in the glossary at the back of the book.

There are a few simple 'guidelines' that I always adhere to when I'm in the kitchen.

Firstly, (instilled in me by my mother!)

Nothing ever went to waste in the kitchen at home. My father was fantastically green-fingered and it was a full-time job for my mother trying to keep up with everything that he grew in our garden ... from grapefruit and guavas to mulberries and macadamias to kumquats, curly kale and crab apples... Fresh produce is so precious and there is a way to make something delicious out of anything (well, almost anything!)

Secondly...

Things really do taste better when they are in season. If we adhere to eating what is in season, we are more likely to be eating locally grown produce than something that has been wrapped in plastic and has flown thousands of miles. In the depths of the winter, I love the anticipation of the summer and the strawberries and asparagus that it brings!

And finally... after twenty-five years of cooking, I am in no doubt as to what 'the secret to success' in the kitchen is:

'Keep it simple'

One of the finest meals I have ever had was in Italy. We sat at a very old wooden table under some ancient apple trees and ate spaghetti with tomatoes, basil and olive oil. Each ingredient was allowed to speak for itself; there was nothing to mask or dull any of the individual flavours; the tomatoes were the sweetest and reddest ones imaginable, the basil was abundantly green and fragrant and the olive oil was 'fresh from the olive', fruity and glistening. We don't need extravagant ingredients to create something special.

My travels as a chef taught me that we also don't need a lavish kitchen and sophisticated equipment to be able to serve up a feast. The skill is in careful planning and in tailoring the menu to the ingredients at your disposal and the facilities available; whether you have a 'Baby Belling' in a kitchen the size of a broom-cupboard or the latest glistening range-cooker in an expansive marble-decked kitchen, it is always possible to create something that will bring a smile to the faces of those you are feeding!

I love cooking for family and friends. There can be no better way to show them how much you care, than feeding them lovingly prepared food! These are the recipes I always use. In the past, some of them have been prepared in a palace kitchen and served to the royal table, while others are favourites from my childhood which I now enjoy making for my daughters and then there are the recipes collected on my travels. Each one really does have a special association for me. My hope is that, using these recipes, you will prepare and serve food that is the centrepiece of many a happy gathering – the type that you will all reminisce about for years to come... big weekend breakfasts that run on 'til well into the afternoon (with gallons of good coffee and a pile of Sunday papers)... long lunches in the garden under sunny summer skies... afternoon tea with cakes to die for ... cosy fireside suppers just for two...

Happy Cooking!

Magnificent Morsels

GREAT LITTLE SNACKS AND NIBBLES

Caprese Tartlets

I nsalata Caprese, my favourite Italian salad, was the inspiration for these little tartlets. It is a simple composition of tomatoes with mozzarella, basil and olive oil. I use baby plum tomatoes, which I bake very slowly to intensify their flavour. The mozzarella is placed onto the tartlets just minutes before they come out of the oven, so that it is warmed through gently, but not cooked. Finally, I spoon a little pesto onto each tartlet after cooking, so that neither the delicate colour, nor the flavour of the basil is impaired by the heat of the oven.

Ingredients

YOU WILL NEED:
One 10cm (4 inch) cutter and two medium baking trays

- 75 mini plum tomatoes * (approximately 2½ US pints)
- 3 sprigs of fresh thyme
- 30ml / 2 Tbsp olive oil
- Salt and freshly ground black pepper
- A sprinkle of caster sugar *
- 1kg / 2lb 4oz ready-made all-butter puff pastry
- 2 balls (250g / 9oz) of good quality buffalo mozzarella chopped into 25 pieces
- 125ml / ½ cup home-made pesto (see recipe on page 111)
- 1 free-range egg (UK medium / USA large) *

* Refer to glossary

Method

Makes 25 tartlets

1. Preheat oven to 150ºC / 300ºF.

2. Prepare the tomatoes. Prick them with a fork and place on a small baking tray with the thyme. Drizzle with olive oil, season with salt and freshly ground black pepper and a sprinkling of caster sugar. Bake for approximately 45 minutes, until they have lost a lot of their juice and look 'shrivelled'. Check them several times during cooking and turn them. Once cooked, keep on one side.

3. Reset the oven to 200ºC / 400ºF.

4. On a lightly floured board, roll out the pastry to approximately 50cm (20 inches) square and to a thickness of about 5mm (¼ inch).

5. Cut out twenty-five 10cm (4 inch) circles.

Continued ➤➤

Method Continued

6. Then using a small sharp knife with a pointy end, cut a second smaller circle (9cm / 4¾ inches in diameter) inside, but do not cut quite all the way round - see diagram below.

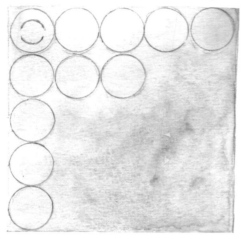

7. Brush the pastry inside the inner circle, with a little water, then fold one half of the cut section over to the opposite side of the circle, as per diagram, repeat by folding the remaining cut section over to the other side.

8. Stick the folded edges down firmly.

9. Place on baking trays and chill for 15 minutes.

10. Beat the egg with a pinch of salt and glaze the rim of each tartlet.

11. Place 3 roasted tomatoes in the centre of each tartlet.

12. Bake for 12 minutes and then reduce the temperature to 180ºC / 350ºF for a further 10 minutes. The tartlets should be well risen and a nice golden colour.

13. Remove from the oven and place a piece of mozzarella on top of the tomatoes in the centre of each tartlet. Return to the oven for just a few minutes to melt the mozzarella.

14. Drizzle a teaspoon of pesto onto each tartlet.

15. Serve immediately.

> "Insalata Caprese, my favourite Italian salad, was the inspiration for these little tartlets."

Crushed Broad Bean
AND GOATS' CHEESE BRUSCHETTA

These summery nibbles have brought a smile to the face of many a vegetarian. When fresh broad beans are not available, frozen ones work just as well. You can ring the changes with the cheese, replacing the goats' cheese with shavings of parmesan or pecorino. They can be transformed into bite-sized canapés by using tiny toasted bread croutes or crisp pastry discs instead of whole slices of baguette. As canapés, they add a lovely splash of colour to a tray of mixed nibbles.

Ingredients

YOU WILL NEED:

One medium baking tray.

- 300g / 10½oz broad beans or lima beans (1¾ cup)
- 30ml / 2 Tbsp extra virgin olive oil
- 15ml / 1 Tbsp fresh lemon juice
- Zest of 1 lemon
- A few sprigs of fresh mint
- 12 slices of baguette
- A little more olive oil
- 115g / 4oz fresh goats' cheese (approx 1 cup)

Method

Makes 12

1. Cook the broad beans in boiling, salted water until tender. Drain, plunge into iced water and peel them. This is a fiddly job, but it is worthwhile doing as the skins can be quite tough and bitter. Also, the colour of the beans is much more vibrant without the skin. (If using lima beans, they don't need to be peeled.)

2. Finely shred the mint.

3. In a mixing bowl, crush the broad beans with the olive oil, lemon juice, lemon zest and shredded mint. Season with salt and freshly ground black pepper.

4. Heat a griddle pan, brush both sides of the bread with a little olive oil and then toast the bread on both sides. If you don't have a griddle pan, you can bake or grill the bread.

5. Pile the crushed broad beans onto the crisped bread. Crumble the goats' cheese and sprinkle a little onto each one of the bruschetta.

6. Serve immediately.

7. A slice of very thin and crispy pancetta laid on top of the cheese, adds a delicious finishing touch for non vegetarians.

Ham, Cheese
AND TOMATO RAREBIT

T his is my interpretation of 'Welsh Rarebit', which is an old, traditional recipe for a hearty slice of toast topped with a cheese sauce made with ale and mustard. My version is much quicker to prepare than the original recipe, and it produces a scrumptious savoury snack. Do use a full flavoured, mature Cheddar cheese rather than a mild one. The mango chutney, which lies concealed beneath the cheese topping, adds a delicious piquancy to this simple treat.

Ingredients

YOU WILL NEED:

One large baking tray

- 6 thick slices bloomer * or sourdough
- 55g / 2oz butter (4 Tbsp)
- 3 spring onions *
- 1 plum tomato
- 200g / 7oz mature Cheddar cheese (1 cup)
- 100g / 3½oz Double Gloucester cheese (½ cup)
- 60g / 2oz honey roast ham
- 15ml / 1 Tbsp finely chopped chives
- 15ml / 1 Tbsp wholegrain mustard
- 75ml / ⅓ cup mayonnaise
- Salt and freshly ground black pepper
- 90ml / 6 Tbsp mango chutney
- A handful of cress or micro-greens

* Refer to glossary

Method

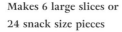

Makes 6 large slices or
24 snack size pieces

1. Preheat the oven to 180ºC / 350ºF.

2. Melt the butter and brush it onto both sides of the sliced bread.

3. Place on a baking sheet and bake for 10–15 minutes to crisp the bread.

4. While the bread is baking, prepare the topping. Slice the spring onions very finely. Peel, seed and dice the plum tomato, grate the cheese and dice the ham. Combine all these ingredients with the chives, mustard and mayonnaise. Season to taste with salt and freshly ground black pepper.

5. When the bread is crisp, spread 1 tablespoon of chutney onto each slice and top with the cheese mixture. Spread it to the edges of the bread.

6. Return to the oven and bake at 200ºC / 400ºF for 15–18 minutes, until golden and bubbling, or it can be grilled.

7. Present as a whole slice or cut it into wedges for a quick snack or bite-sized morsels to serve as canapés.

8. Sprinkle with cress or micro-greens and serve immediately.

Parmesan
AND FRESH HERB RISOTTO BALLS

Ingredients

FOR THE RISOTTO:

- 500ml / 2¼ cups chicken or vegetable stock *
- 1 clove garlic
- 1 small leek
- 3 shallots
- 30g / 1oz butter (2 Tbsp)
- 30 ml / 2 Tbsp olive oil
- 200g / 7oz Carnaroli or Arborio rice * (⅔ cup)
- 150ml / ⅔ cup dry white wine
- 50g / 2oz freshly grated parmesan (½ cup)
- 30g / 1oz crème fraîche (⅛ cup)
- A handful of basil leaves
- A handful of wild rocket leaves *
- 15ml / 1 Tbsp finely chopped chives
- 1 ball buffalo mozzarella (125g / 4½oz)

TO CRUMB THE RISOTTO BALLS:

- 50g / 2oz plain flour * (½ cup)
- 2 free-range eggs, beaten (UK medium / USA large) *
- 150g / 6oz fresh breadcrumbs (1½ cups)
- 1 litre / 3½ cups sunflower oil

* Refer to glossary

Method

Makes about 30

1. Place the stock in a large saucepan and bring to a gentle simmer.

2. Meanwhile, crush the garlic. Wash the leek and finely chop it with the shallots.

3. Melt the butter and oil in a heavy-based saucepan and sauté the garlic, leek and shallots until soft and translucent but not coloured.

4. Stir in the rice and cook for a couple of minutes.

5. Add the wine and continue stirring until most of it has evaporated.

6. Add the hot stock, ladle by ladle, to the rice mixture and cook for about 15 minutes, or longer, according to the cooking instructions of rice you are using. Stir continuously.

7. When still just *al dente*, remove from the heat and add the cheese and crème fraîche and season to taste. Leave to cool for a few minutes.

8. Tear the basil leaves and roughly chop the rocket, and stir them into the risotto with the chives.

9. Pour the risotto into a tray that you have lined with a silicon sheet or cling film*, leave to cool completely.

10. Divide the mozzarella into 30 small pieces.

11. Shape the risotto into balls the size of a walnut. Press a cube of mozzarella into the centre of each one.

12. Coat each ball in flour, then the beaten egg, and breadcrumbs. Chill thoroughly.

13. Heat the oil in a deep heavy-based pan and fry the risotto balls a few at a time to a golden colour with crisp shell.

14. Drain on absorbent kitchen paper and serve immediately.

U sing this recipe, you can transform risotto into finger food! These little risotto balls, crispy on the outside with a molten, cheesy centre, are heavenly. Large risotto balls make an irresistible starter; serve them with a chunky tomato sauce or creamed spinach. This recipe is a great way to use up left-over risotto.

Mini Roast Chicken
AND LEEK PIES

T his recipe calls for a roasted chicken breast for the filling, but if you have some left-over roast chicken in your refrigerator then use that instead. If leeks are not in season, then combine asparagus, sweet corn or mushrooms with the chicken.

Ingredients

YOU WILL NEED:

Twelve 5cm (2inch) tartlet moulds or a 12-hole muffin tin.

FOR THE SEEDY PASTRY:

- 115g / 4oz butter (1 stick)
- 225g / 8oz plain flour * (2 cups)
- A generous pinch of salt
- 15ml / 1 Tbsp pine nuts *
- 10ml / 2 tsp sesame seeds
- 5ml / 1 tsp poppy seeds
- 60ml / 4 Tbsp water
- 1 free-range egg yolk (UK medium / USA large) *

FOR THE FILLING:

- 1 roasted chicken breast (150g / 5oz)
- 1 large leek (approximately 150g / 5oz)
- 30g / 1oz butter (2 Tbsp)
- 2 sprigs of fresh thyme
- Zest of 1 lemon
- 100ml / 7 Tbsp crème fraîche
- 1 free-range egg yolk (UK medium / USA large) *
- Salt and freshly ground black pepper
- 1 free-range egg (UK medium / USA large) *

* Refer to glossary

Method

Makes 12 mini pies

1. Make the pastry: Using a food processor, process the butter, flour, salt and pine nuts together until they resemble fine breadcrumbs. Alternatively, you can rub this in by hand.

2. Add the seeds. Then mix the egg yolk and water and slowly add this while the food processor is running. You may not need all the liquid.

3. When the dough is almost mixed, but is still not drawn together in one smooth ball, turn it out onto a floured board and bring it together by hand. (If you over-process it, you will have tough, hard pastry)

4. Wrap in cling film* and leave to rest in the refrigerator for 20 minutes while you make the filling.

5. Dice the roast chicken in 1cm (½ inch) cubes.

6. Finely chop the leeks and cook them in the butter until tender. Mix in the diced chicken, a sprinkling of fresh thyme leaves, the crème fraîche and egg yolk and grate the lemon zest into the mixture. Season with salt and freshly ground black pepper. Leave to chill in the refrigerator.

7. Roll out the pastry to a thickness of 5mm (¼ inch). Cut out twelve 6cm (2¼ inch) circles for the base of the pies and twelve 3-4cm (1-1½ inch) circles for the top of each pie (depending on the exact size of the mould you are using).

8. Set the oven to 200ºC / 400ºF.

9. Line each mould with pastry, pushing it well down into the corners. Fill each little pie generously with the chicken mixture.

10. Brush the underside of each of the pie tops with a little water, to stick them on to the base, so that the filling does not ooze out during cooking.

11. Beat the egg with a pinch of salt and use it to glaze the top of each little pie.

12. Bake for 20 minutes or until the pastry is golden and crisp.

Pancetta-Wrapped
BABY NEW POTATOES
SERVED WITH APPLE CHUTNEY

These are my favourite 'Magnificent Morsels'. They are pure simplicity, with just four ingredients and the bare minimum of preparation required. If you are having a barbecue, cook some of these over the coals to stave off the pangs of hunger while you are waiting for the sausages and other bigger items to cook.

Ingredients

YOU WILL NEED:

One medium baking tray and some cocktail sticks or toothpicks

- 24 baby new potatoes
- 60ml / 4 Tbsp virgin olive oil
- 60ml / 4 Tbsp finely grated parmesan
- 24 very thin slices of pancetta or very thin streaky bacon

TO SERVE:

- Apple chutney (see recipe on page 249)
- A handful of sprigs of Greek basil

Method

Makes 24

1. Cook the new potatoes in boiling salted water until tender.

2. Roll the potatoes in the olive oil and then in the grated parmesan.

3. Wrap each potato in a rasher of pancetta, and secure each one with a cocktail stick.

4. Place on baking tray making sure that the 'join' is underneath (otherwise the pancetta will unravel during cooking). Bake at 200ºC / 400ºF for 12 – 15 minutes.

5. Serve immediately, with the basil scattered on the serving platter, accompanied by chutney for dipping.

Salmon
MAYONNAISE WRAPS

I am always on the look-out for good ways to use up left-overs and these healthy little nibbles are perfect for using up left-over cold salmon. Alternatively, you can quickly and easily poach or bake a piece of salmon. I blend a handful of gorgeous fresh herbs into some mayonnaise. The pale green mayonnaise contrasts beautifully with the pink salmon. Using lettuce as a wrap, rather than a flatbread, makes these very light and summery. For a lunch-sized portion wrap the salmon in a large lettuce leaf, such as Cos or Romaine.

Ingredients

- 225g / 8oz cold poached salmon

FOR THE GREEN MAYONNAISE:
- 100g / 3½oz mayonnaise (½ cup)
- Zest of 1 lemon
- A handful of rocket * and mint leaves
- Sea salt
- Freshly ground black pepper

TO ASSEMBLE:
- 24 small 'Little Gem' lettuce leaves *
- 24 tiny sprigs of dill

* Refer to glossary

Method

Makes 24

1. Using a hand blender, combine all the ingredients for the green mayonnaise. Blend until you have a smooth textured, delicate green mayonnaise.

2. Season to taste with salt and freshly ground black pepper.

3. Flake the salmon and mix it into the mayonnaise.

4. Wash the lettuce leaves and dry them thoroughly.

5. Place a teaspoonful of salmon mayonnaise into each lettuce leaf.

6. Garnish each one with a sprig of dill.

7. Serve immediately.

Spinach
AND FETA CHEESE TRIANGLES

Ingredients

YOU WILL NEED:

One medium baking tray

FOR THE FILLING:

- 400g / 14oz spinach
- 1 onion
- 30ml / 2 Tbsp olive oil
- 30g / 1oz toasted pine nuts * (¼ cup)
- 85g / 3oz crumbled feta cheese (¾ cup)
- Freshly grated black pepper
- A little nutmeg

FOR THE PASTRY:

- 4 large sheets of filo pastry 48cm x 25cm (19 x 10 inches)
- 55g / 2oz melted butter (4 Tbsp)

FOR THE DIPPING SAUCE:

- 200ml / ¾ cup thick Greek yoghurt
- A handful of fresh mint, finely chopped
- Zest of 1 lemon
- A fine sprinkling of paprika

Method

Makes 12 small triangles

1. Wash, drain and cook the spinach. Squeeze out as much moisture as possible then chop it finely.

2. Chop the onion finely and sauté it in the olive oil until it is soft and translucent.

3. Mix together the spinach, onion, pine nuts and feta cheese. Season with pepper and nutmeg.

4. Lay one sheet of filo on a pastry board and paint it all over with melted butter. Top with a second sheet and more butter. Cover the remaining sheets of pastry with a slightly damp tea towel to prevent them from drying out and cracking.

5. Cut the buttered filo pastry along the length into 6 strips, each 8cm (3¼ inches) wide.

6. In the top corner of each strip place a spoonful of the spinach filling.

7. Fold the pastry across diagonally to form a little triangle. Continue folding it all the way down to the bottom of the strip of filo, so that you have neat little triangle (like a samosa).

8. Repeat with the remaining 5 strips and then start the process again from the beginning with the remaining two sheets of filo pastry.

9. Bake at 200ºC / 400ºF for 10 minutes, then reduce the temperature to 180ºC / 350ºF for 12–15 minutes.

10. For the dipping sauce: Mix all the ingredients, saving a bit of the mint and lemon zest to sprinkle on top as a garnish.

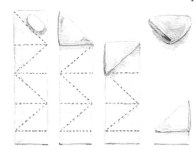

Fold the pastry across diagonally to form a little triangle. Continue folding it all the way down to the bottom of the strip of filo, so that you have neat little triangle (like a samosa).

I tasted some incredibly good little spinach pastries in a market in Istanbul, when I was there on an official visit with HRH The Prince of Wales. This is my attempt to replicate them. I wish I could also recreate the wonderful heady aroma of the spice section of the Turkish market, which I am sure contributed to them tasting so very good!

A Superb Sandwich

What makes a sandwich superb? Home-made or freshly baked bread is a must; I use my home-made soda bread. You should be generous with quantity of filling that you use and discerning about what goes into the filling. All good sandwiches should include 'crisp' or 'crunchy' elements such as cucumber or toasted seeds. Also, they need something that keeps the sandwich deliciously moist and 'sticks it together' such as mayonnaise, hummus, tapenade, cream cheese or pesto. Always remember to season your sandwich filling, especially salad. I keep my salt and pepper mills to hand and season the layers as I build them up. You can create a sandwich with plenty of height, by carefully stacking up the filling.

Ingredients

- 3 thin rashers * smoked streaky bacon
- 2 slices of soda bread (see recipe on page 220)
- 15ml / 1 Tbsp soft butter
- 30ml / 2 Tbsp home-made pesto (see recipe on page 111)
- 15ml / 1 Tbsp mayonnaise
- 2 sundried tomatoes (in oil)
- A few slices of avocado
- 1 Tbsp olive oil
- Juice of ½ a lemon
- 12 large shavings of parmesan
- 15ml / 1 Tbsp toasted pine nuts *
- A few slices of cucumber
- A few slices of tomato
- 1 Tbsp fine alfalfa sprouts
- A handful of wild rocket leaves *
- Salt and freshly ground black pepper

* Refer to glossary

Method

Makes 1 sandwich

1. Cook the bacon until it is crisp.
2. Butter the bread.
3. Spread one slice with half of the pesto and the other slice with the mayonnaise.
4. Dice the sundried tomato and sprinkle it onto the mayonnaise.
5. Mix the avocado with olive oil and lemon juice and season with salt and pepper.
6. Layer up all the ingredients, in any order, using several layers of parmesan.
7. Season with salt and pepper and drizzle with the remaining pesto as you go.
8. Top with the second slice of bread and cut in half to serve. Carefully wrapped, this is perfect picnic food.

Mushroom Tartlets

Ingredients

YOU WILL NEED:

One medium baking tray

FOR THE TARTLET BASES:

- 1kg / 2lb 4oz ready-made all-butter puff pastry
- 1 free-range egg (UK medium / USA large) *

FOR THE MUSHROOM CREAM:

- 20g / ½oz dried porcini *
- 2 onions
- 60ml / 4 Tbsp olive oil
- 300g / 10½oz mixed woodland mushrooms or chestnut mushrooms *
- 5ml / 1 tsp fresh thyme leaves
- A squeeze of fresh lemon juice
- 45ml / 3 Tbsp cream
- 1 egg yolk
- 5ml / 1 tsp finely chopped chives
- Salt and freshly ground black pepper

FOR THE TOPPING:

- 200g / 7oz chestnut mushrooms *
- 15g / ½oz butter
- A squeeze of fresh lemon juice
- Seasoning
- 15ml / 1 Tbsp finely chopped chives

* Refer to glossary

Method

Makes 20 small tarts

1. Roll out the pastry out on a floured board to a thickness of 5mm (¼ inch).

2. Cut out twenty small rectangles, approximately 5cm x 10cm (2 inches x 4 inches) and place them on a baking tray.

3. Beat the egg with pinch of salt, glaze the tartlets and chill them.

4. Soak the dried porcini in a little water to reconstitute them. When soft, drain and chop them.

5. Make the mushroom cream: Finely dice the onion and sauté it in 2 tablespoons of olive oil until soft and lightly coloured, remove from the pan.

6. Sauté the woodland mushrooms and the porcini in the remaining olive oil until tender and lightly coloured. Add the thyme and season with salt, pepper and lemon juice. Mix with the onions.

7. Blend the mixture to a 'paste' using a blender or food processor.

8. Add the cream, egg yolk and chives. Leave to cool.

9. For the topping: Slice and then sauté the chestnut mushrooms in the butter, add lemon juice, a pinch of salt and a twist of freshly ground black pepper.

10. To assemble the tartlets: Spread 2 tablespoons of mushroom cream along the centre of each rectangle of pastry and arrange the sliced chestnut mushrooms on top.

11. Bake at 220ºC / 425ºF for 15 minutes.

12. Sprinkle with finely chopped chives and serve hot straight from the oven.

Left: An extract from a note to me from HRH The Prince of Wales

A million thanks for being such a Stars... with immense gratitude from Charles

When you bite into these tartlets you will find a deliciously rich and creamy filling concealed beneath the decorative mushrooms on the top. I love to cook with wild mushrooms; they are attractive and flavoursome. However, they are seasonal. When they are not available, I substitute chestnut mushrooms with the addition of some dried porcini to give the filling a robust flavour. You can make the tartlets in any shape, but this shape is easy to bite into.

Beautiful Beginnings

FIRST COURSES AND SOUPS

W henever I cook with asparagus, I always remember the perfect asparagus that was grown at Highgrove, HRH The Prince of Wales's country residence. Asparagus was only ever on the menu when it was growing in the garden. The traditional season for asparagus in England runs from St George's Day to Midsummer's Eve (April 23rd to June 21st). Asparagus remains a wonderful treat when it is keenly anticipated for 44 weeks of the year and eaten with relish during these eight weeks only!

Asparagus & New Potato Soup
WITH PARMESAN STRAWS

Ingredients

FOR THE PARMESAN STRAWS:
(Makes 18)

- 200g / 7oz ready-made, all-butter puff pastry
- 1 free-range egg (UK medium / USA large) *
- 30ml / 2 Tbsp finely chopped chives
- 45ml / 3 Tbsp finely grated parmesan

- 5ml / 1 tsp white sesame seeds
- 5ml / 1 tsp black sesame seeds
- A pinch of paprika

FOR THE SOUP:

- 800g / 1¾ lb asparagus (about 50 spears)
- 2 medium onions
- 1 small leek
- 30ml / 2 Tbsp olive oil
- 750ml / 3 cups tasty chicken stock *

- 150ml / ⅔ cup crème fraîche
- 15ml / 1 Tbsp finely chopped chives
- Salt & freshly ground black pepper

FOR THE GARNISH:

- The asparagus tips from the 800g asparagus
- 6 small new potatoes
- 30g / 1oz butter (2 Tbsp)
- A handful of fresh chervil

* Refer to glossary

Method

**Makes 4 generous 'lunch-time' servings
or 6 starter-size servings**

1. Make the parmesan straws: Roll out the pastry on a floured board to a size of 25cm (10 inches) square and a thickness of 3mm (⅛ inch). Glaze all over with the egg and sprinkle with the chives, parmesan, sesame seeds and paprika. Chill for 10 minutes in the refrigerator (this makes the pastry much easier to cut) then, using a long-bladed knife, cut 18 long points as shown in the diagram, then chill again.

2. Preheat the oven to 190ºC / 375ºF and bake the straws for 12 – 15 minutes.

3. Make the soup: Snap off and discard the tough, woody bottom section of the asparagus stalks. Cut off the tips to use for the garnish. Chop the remaining stalks into 1cm (½ inch) sections.

4. Peel and finely dice the onions, wash and finely chop the leek. Cook them slowly in the olive oil in a heavy based pan over a low heat with a lid on, until the onion is translucent and the leek is very soft. Don't allow them to brown as this will spoil the colour of the soup.

5. Bring the chicken stock to the boil in another pan. Cook the asparagus tips in the stock for 3–5 minutes until tender, plunge them into cold water, drain and keep on one side.

6. Dice the new potatoes, cook them in the stock until tender, drain and keep on one side.

7. Once the onion and leek are soft, add the chicken stock and asparagus stems to the pan. Cook for 10-12 minutes until the asparagus is tender. Don't overcook or the asparagus becomes a very dull colour.

8. Remove from the heat and cool before blending it to a silky smooth consistency using a liquidiser or a stick blender.

9. To serve the soup, reheat it thoroughly. Whisk in the crème fraîche and chives, add salt and pepper to taste.

10. Meanwhile, reheat the asparagus tips and diced new potato in the butter.

11. Pour the soup into pre-warmed cups or bowls and top with a spoon of diced potato, a few asparagus tips and a pretty sprig of chervil. Serve with a couple of parmesan straws.

Crab Tian
WITH MANGO AND AVOCADO

If you are looking for a starter that takes next to no time to prepare and yet will still impress your guests, then this is the one for you. It is also versatile; while it is perfect for a light summer's lunch, it is certainly not out of place served at a formal dinner. You can vary the presentation and if you don't have ring moulds, then you can shape the crab into quenelles using two tablespoons. If you are preparing this more than an hour before it will be served, leave out the avocado as it will become discoloured. In this case you could use diced tomato instead and garnish with avocado and superfine beans.

Ingredients

YOU WILL NEED:

Four 10cm (4 inch) metal rings that are at least 5cm (2 inches) high OR you can use ramekins of similar size.

FOR THE CRAB MAYONNAISE:

- 400g / 14oz white crab meat
- Zest of 1 lemon
- 1 red chilli
- 6 spring onions *
- 75ml / ⅓ cup mayonnaise
- Sea salt and freshly ground black pepper
- A handful of fresh mint leaves
- 1 large ripe avocado
- A squeeze of fresh lemon juice

FOR THE GARNISH:

- 1 large ripe but firm avocado
- A squeeze of fresh lemon juice
- A drizzle of extra virgin olive oil
- Sea salt and freshly ground black pepper
- 1 ripe mango
- A handful of wild rocket *
- A few extra mint leaves

* Refer to glossary

Method

Serves 4

1. Line the rings or ramekins with cling film* and chill in the refrigerator.

2. For the crab mayonnaise: Check the crab meat carefully with your fingers and remove any small pieces of shell. Finely grate the lemon zest into the crabmeat. Seed and finely slice the chilli and chop the spring onions very thinly, mix both into the crabmeat with the mayonnaise. Season delicately with salt and freshly ground black pepper.

3. Lastly, shred the mint and mix it into the crab mayonnaise.

4. Divide half the crab mayonnaise between the 4 rings or moulds.

5. Dice one of the avocados, squeeze the lemon juice over it and season with salt and pepper.

6. Place a quarter of the diced avocado into each ring and distribute it evenly over the crab.

7. Cover the avocado with the remaining crab mayonnaise. Press down well so that the tian holds its shape when turned out.

8. Chill for at least 30 minutes.

9. Turn each tian out onto the centre of a plate and surround with small chunks of mango and avocado and a few mint leaves.

10. Drizzle the lemon juice and olive oil over the mango and avocado. Season with black pepper and finish with a little twist of wild rocket on top of each tian.

Pea & Ham Risotto

I learnt to make risotto in Italy – the Italian way. I shall always treasure the memories of this particular culinary adventure as it was punctuated with more gesticulating and laughter than I have ever experienced in any other kitchen. My lack of command of Italian did not seem to hinder my progress in learning the finer points of this wonderful cuisine; the chefs were kind, funny and keen to share their vast knowledge. In this recipe, I have introduced a very 'English' pairing of ingredients – peas and ham – into risotto, one of the great cornerstones of Italian gastronomy. I love the vibrant colours and delicate flavours of this combination.

There are some wonderfully evocative Italian terms for the various stages of making a risotto...

Soffrito is the sautéed garlic and onion to which the rice is added.

Tostatura is the process of cooking the rice in the garlic, onion and butter to coat each grain with a film of fat.

Mantecatura is the vigorous beating in of butter and parmesan just before serving to give the risotto a silky richness and to make it 'all'onde' – 'flow in waves'

Ingredients

- 340g / 12oz frozen peas (2 cups)
- A handful of sugar snaps *
- 115g / 4oz unsalted butter * (1 stick)
- 1 small leek
- 1 onion
- 1 clove of garlic
- 225g / 8oz Carnaroli risotto rice * (1 cup)
- 225ml / 1 cup dry white wine
- 1 litre / 4½ cups chicken stock *
- 60g / 2oz freshly grated parmesan (½ cup)
- 115g / 4oz diced ham (¾ cup)
- 4 sprigs of mint
- 60ml / 4 Tbsp crème fraîche

* Refer to glossary

Method

Serves 4, generously

1. Cook the frozen peas in boiling, salted water until tender. Do not overcook as they will lose their vibrant green colour. Drain and reserve a little of the water they were cooked in.

2. Set aside ¼ cup of the peas. Using a stick blender or liquidiser, blend the remaining peas to a smooth purée, adding about 4 tablespoons of the cooking water and 30g (2 tablespoons) of butter. Season with salt and freshly ground black pepper. Keep on one side.

3. Cook the sugar snaps lightly, so that they are still crisp, and set aside with the remaining peas, to use for garnishing the risotto.

4. Remove the tough outer layers from the leek, then chop it finely. If it is at all muddy, place it in a colander or sieve and rinse it under cold running water, drain well.

5. Peel and finely chop the onion and crush the garlic.

6. In a heavy-based, deep saucepan melt 45g (3 tablespoons) of the butter and add the onion, leek and garlic. Cook until it is very soft and starting to colour. This is your *soffrito*.

7. Add the rice to the *soffrito* and stir well.

Continued ➤

"I learnt to make risotto in Italy – the Italian way. I will always treasure the memories of this particular culinary adventure as it was punctuated with more gesticulating and laughter than I have ever experienced in any other kitchen."

Method Continued

8. Next, the *tostatura* stage: Cook the rice gently with the buttery onions and garlic for a couple of minutes to ensure that each grain is coated in butter.

9. Add the white wine and cook rapidly. Continue stirring until the liquid has mostly evaporated.

10. Bring the stock to a simmer in a separate saucepan.

11. Add the stock to the rice ladle by ladle. Cook over a low heat, stirring constantly. Once most of the stock has been absorbed, add the next ladleful.

12. It is important to keep stirring the rice as this helps to release its starchy coating while also allowing the harder kernel to gently swell and soften, and it is this that gives the risotto its silky texture.

13. Carnaroli rice will take 15–18 minutes to cook. Arborio may take a bit longer. Check the package instructions for precise timings.

14. Taste the risotto from time to time to see if the rice is tender. Traditionally, it should be served with a little bit of 'bite' to it. You may not need to use all of the stock.

15. Add the pea purée, peas, sugar snaps and diced ham to the risotto. Heat it through quickly, but do not cook for too long or the colour will lose its vibrancy. The risotto should 'flow', it should be 'all onde'. If it doesn't slip off a spoon easily, then add more hot stock to it.

16. You have now reached the *mantecatura* stage: Vigorously stir in the remaining butter and all but 2 tablespoons of the parmesan, for a wonderfully creamy finish to the risotto.

17. Spoon a dollop of crème fraîche onto the risotto. Finely chop the mint and sprinkle it on top with the remaining parmesan. Serve at once.

Nov. 26th 1991.

Carolyn —
That was a memorable
lunch today! I have
rarely had such a
delicious one and I cannot
begin to congratulate you
enough for producing
such a wonderful
example of the culinary
arts!

Charles

Receiving a note like this always served to remind me that I really did
have the best job in the world; I was doing what I loved most of all and
I had the most incredible 'boss' that anyone could wish for.

T his is comfort food at its best. I have served this dish for breakfast, for lunch, for an informal supper and as the starter for a formal dinner. The plates always come back almost licked clean. The combination of bacon and eggs is an age-old winner and in this dish the addition of wonderful crushed new potatoes and home-made pesto augment it to a thoroughly sublime plate of food. For the very best poached eggs use fresh, locally produced organic eggs.

Poached Egg on Crushed New Potatoes

WITH PEA SHOOTS, CRISPY BACON AND BASIL SAUCE

Ingredients

YOU WILL NEED:

Four metal rings, approximately 10cm (4 inches) in diameter, and a medium baking tray. If you don't have rings, you can make 'free-form' potato cakes.

FOR THE CRUSHED NEW POTATOES:

- 600g / 1 lb 6oz new potatoes
- 45ml / 3 Tbsp cream
- 50g / 2oz butter (4 Tbsp)
- Salt and freshly ground black pepper
- A pinch of ground nutmeg
- 4 free-range eggs (UK medium / USA large) *
- A splash of vinegar

FOR THE SAUCE:

- 200ml / ¾ cup cream
- 60ml / 4 Tbsp home-made pesto (see recipe on page 111)

FOR THE GARNISH:

- 8 thin slices smoked streaky bacon
- 20 shavings of parmesan
- 16 - 20 pea shoots

* Refer to glossary

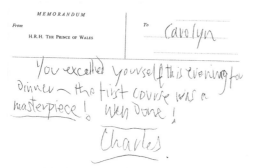

MEMORANDUM

From H.R.H. THE PRINCE OF WALES   To Carolyn

You excelled yourself this evening for Dinner — the first course was a masterpiece! Well Done!

Charles

Method

Serves 4

1. Cook the new potatoes in boiling salted water until tender, drain.

2. Heat the cream and butter together, add the potatoes and roughly crush them into the cream, using a fork; they do not need to be completely mashed, leave them quite chunky. Season to taste with salt, pepper and nutmeg.

3. Divide the crushed potato between the 4 metal rings and keep warm in the oven.

4. Cook the eggs in an egg poacher. Alternatively, add a splash of vinegar to approximately 10cm (4 inches) of gently simmering water in a small saucepan. Break one of the eggs into a small bowl. Stir the water in a clockwise direction to create a current, then carefully slip the egg into the centre of the pan. The swirling water will help to keep the egg together in a small compact shape. When the egg is cooked and firm (this takes about 2 minutes) remove with a slotted spoon and keep on one side in another pan filled with hot water. Repeat with the next 3 eggs. Keep on one side, in hot water, until needed.

5. Either grill or fry the bacon until crispy.

6. Bring the cream to the boil and then whisk in the pesto.

7. To serve: Place a couple of spoonfuls of sauce onto the centre of each warmed plate. Put the crushed potato cakes onto the sauce and top with a few pea shoots.

8. Finish with the poached eggs and place two pieces of crispy bacon on top of each egg.

9. Toss the parmesan shavings onto the plate and serve immediately.

A very special note of thanks from His Royal Highness. He broke his right arm while playing polo but that didn't stop him from writing — he used his left hand instead!

Roasted Butternut & Corn Soup
SERVED WITH SOUR CREAM, CRUNCHY TORTILLA STRIPS AND AVOCADO

Roasting the butternut for this hearty soup, creates a deliciously full-bodied flavour and a texture that is thick and velvety. If you can lay your hands on some fresh chicken stock, use that rather than stock cubes, which are generally very salty and will mask the delicate flavour of the butternut. Crunchy tortilla strips make a welcome change from serving croutons. The avocado and sour cream add lovely fresh colours and a touch of indulgence to this soup.

Ingredients

YOU WILL NEED:
A Roasting tray, 1 baking tray, 6 soup bowls & 18 small china, ceramic or wooden bowls

FOR THE SOUP:
- 1kg / 2lb 3oz butternut, (a butternut of 1.2kg / 2lb 7oz will yield this)
- 2 large white onions
- Olive oil
- Salt & freshly ground black pepper

- A pinch or 2 of chilli powder
- 30ml / 2 Tbsp brown sugar
- 115g / 4oz frozen or tinned sweet corn *
- 1 litre / 4½ cups chicken stock *
- 225ml / 1 cup milk

GARNISH:
- 1 avocado
- 2 corn tortillas
- 180ml / ¾ cup sour cream

Method

Serves 6

1. Preheat the oven to 200ºC / 400ºF.

2. Peel the butternut, remove the seeds and dice it into 5cm (2 inch) cubes. Peel and slice the onions. Place the butternut and onions in a roasting tin, sprinkle with olive oil, salt, freshly ground black pepper, chilli powder and brown sugar. Toss everything together.

3. Roast for 20 minutes then toss the butternut and onion again. Turn the oven down to 180ºC / 350ºF and cook for a further 30 minutes, checking from time to time and turning them so that they cook evenly.

4. While the vegetables are roasting, prepare the garnish: Dice the avocado, mix it with a little olive oil, lemon juice, salt and freshly ground black pepper. Divide it between 6 small bowls or small plates.

5. Roll the tortillas and slice them at 5mm (¼ inch) intervals. Heat a baking sheet with a splash of olive oil on it, place the tortilla pieces onto it, bake for about 10 minutes or until golden. Divide between 6 small bowls or small plates.

6. Place 2 tablespoons of soured cream in each of 6 small bowls, keep chilled.

7. If using frozen sweet corn, cook and drain it. If using tinned sweet corn just drain it.

8. When the butternut and onion are soft and lightly coloured they are ready. Warm the chicken stock in a large saucepan and add the roasted vegetables to it. Using either a stick blender or a liquidiser, blend the soup to a velvety smooth purée.

9. Return soup to the pan, add the milk and corn and taste to check the seasoning.

10. To serve, reheat the soup thoroughly. When it is piping hot, ladle it into pre-warmed soup bowls. Accompany each bowl of soup with the 3 tiny bowls, containing the diced avocado, sour cream and crisp tortilla strips.

Salad Of Prosciutto-Wrapped Peaches
WITH FIGS AND BUFFALO MOZZARELLA

I t is always good to have a recipe up your sleeve that can be put together in a matter of minutes. This salad is extremely quick to prepare. However it is definitely a summer dish, to be made when juicy peaches are at their sweet and succulent best. When peaches are not in season, try combining pears with crispy prosciutto and crumbled Rocquefort cheese. An aged Balsamic vinegar and a fruity olive oil complement the stronger flavours of this salad perfectly.

Ingredients

- 50g / 2oz pecan halves (½ cup)
- 30ml / 2 Tbsp light olive oil
- Salt, pepper, brown sugar & chilli powder
- 2 large, perfectly ripe yellow peaches
- 12 slices of prosciutto
- 4 ripe figs
- 2 balls of buffalo mozzarella (250g / 9oz)
- A handful of washed wild rocket *
- 120ml / 8 Tbsp walnut oil
- 60ml / 4 Tbsp raspberry vinegar
- Freshly ground black pepper
- Freshly milled sea salt

* Refer to glossary

Method

Serves 4

1. To prepare the spiced pecans, place them on a baking tray, drizzle the oil over them and sprinkle with salt, pepper, sugar and chilli powder. Shake the tray to distribute the seasoning evenly. Bake at 170ºC / 325ºF for 12 – 15 minutes. Leave to cool.

2. Cut each peach into 6 segments. I leave the skin on, but you can peel them for those who don't like the 'furry-ness' of peach skin.

3. Wrap one piece of prosciutto around each segment of peach.

4. Cut each fig into 3 segments.

5. Tear each mozzarella ball into 6 pieces.

6. Arrange 3 pieces each of peach, fig and mozzarella alternately around each plate in a circle.

7. Place a little bundle of rocket leaves in the centre.

8. Sprinkle on a few spiced pecans.

9. Spoon a little walnut oil and then the raspberry vinegar over the salad.

10. Finish with a twist of black pepper and a twist of salt. Serve immediately.

Light & Summery

MAIN COURSES FOR
SUNNY DAYS AND BALMY NIGHTS

*T*he crust of this tart does more than just hold the filling in place – it is delicious in its own right. I use half malted granary flour, some of my favourite seeds and fresh thyme and chives in the pastry, which give it plenty of texture, colour and flavour. If you are in a hurry you can use pre-prepared pastry, but nothing can surpass home-made pastry.

Asparagus, Swiss Chard
AND GOATS' CHEESE TART

Ingredients

YOU WILL NEED:

One 23cm (9 inch) metal flan ring or fluted loose bottomed flan tin, ceramic baking beans. *

FOR THE PASTRY:

- 115g / 4oz cold butter (1 stick)
- 85g / 3oz plain flour * (⅔ cup)
- 85g / 3oz malted granary flour * (⅔ cup)
- 5ml / 1 tsp linseed *
- 5ml / 1 tsp poppy seeds
- 5ml / 1 tsp pumpkin seeds
- 1 free-range egg yolk (UK medium / USA large) *
- 20ml / 4 tsp cold water
- Pinch of salt
- 1 tsp finely chopped chives
- ½ tsp fresh thyme leaves

FOR THE FILLING:

- 20 spears of asparagus, (approx 500g / 1lb 2oz)
- 150g / 5oz Swiss chard
- 2 large shallots
- 55g / 2oz finely grated parmesan (½ cup)
- 125g / 4oz goats' cheese log with a bloomy rind
- 200ml / ¾ cup double cream *
- 200ml / ¾ cup crème fraîche
- 3 free-range eggs (UK medium / USA large) *
- Salt, pepper and nutmeg
- Paprika and a handful of pine nuts *

* Refer to glossary

Method

Serves 6

1. For the pastry: Put all the ingredients into a food processor. Using the 'pulse' button, process until the mixture resembles chunky breadcrumbs. (To make by hand: Mix the flour, seeds, salt and herbs. Rub in the butter, then mix in the egg and water). Tip the mixture onto a lightly floured surface and bring it together with the hands to form a smooth ball, working as lightly as possible.

2. On a lightly floured board, roll out the pastry into a circle of approximately 36cm (14 inches) diameter and to a thickness of 5mm (¼ inch). Line the flan ring with the pastry, leaving the pastry standing at least 1cm (½ inch) above the top of the tin, to allow for shrinkage when it cooks. If you use scissors to trim the top it is less likely to shrink down. Chill for at least 20 minutes before baking.

3. Preheat the oven to 200ºC / 400ºF.

4. Line the flan with baking parchment or foil and fill it with ceramic baking beans. Bake for 15 minutes then remove the beans and bake for a further 5 – 10 minutes to crisp up the base.

5. For the filling: Prepare the asparagus by snapping off the woody end sections of the stems and discarding them, then cut off the tips and keep to one side. Cut the remainder of the stems into 5cm (2 inch) lengths. Cook the tips lightly in boiling salted water, then remove and cook the stems, which will take a little longer. Chill in cold water when cooked, drain and keep on one side.

6. Wash the Swiss chard. Remove the coarse stems. Blanch the leaves in boiling, salted water for just a few seconds, or longer if the leaves are large and coarse. Drain well.

7. Chop the shallots very finely and place them in the base of the tart. Sprinkle with half of the parmesan, then lay the asparagus and chard on top, finish with the remaining parmesan.

8. Slice the goats' cheese log into 9 rounds and arrange them on the top of the asparagus and chard.

9. Whisk together the cream, crème fraîche and eggs. Season with a pinch of salt and nutmeg and a few twists of black pepper and pour over the tart. Sprinkle with pine nuts and dust with paprika.

10. Bake at 190ºC / 375ºF for 30 minutes or until the filling is set and the top is golden in colour. Serve warm.

Curried Chicken Salad
WITH FRESH MANGO & TOASTED CASHEWS

This is my interpretation of Coronation chicken, a dish that was created especially for Her Majesty The Queen's Coronation celebrations in June 1953. When I make this, it always brings back fond memories of the many buffet lunches that I prepared aboard HMY Britannia (the Royal Yacht). It was a favourite to put on the menu when we had a large number of guests to feed, particularly when we were in a hot climate. My most memorable lunch was one when the Britannia was at anchor right next to Tower Bridge in London on a beautiful summer's day. Wherever in the world we were, when we were on board the royal yacht it felt as if we had brought a tiny corner of Britain with us. It had a wonderful feel to it and it always looked very spectacular, with each last tiny piece of brass detail glistening, the paintwork totally immaculate, every corner of wooden deck scrubbed until it was pristine and a fantastically colourful array of flags and ensigns flapping in the breeze.

Ingredients

FOR THE SAUCE:
- 45ml / 3 Tbsp curry powder
- 30ml / 2 Tbsp honey
- 45ml / 3 Tbsp white wine
- 60ml / 4 Tbsp mango chutney
- 225ml / 1 cup mayonnaise
- 100ml / ½ cup double cream *
- 4 cooked chicken breasts (approximately 650g / 1lb 7oz)

FOR THE MIXED GRAIN SALAD:
- 225g / 8oz mixed bulgur wheat and red and white quinoa (1½ cups)
- ½ sweet red pepper
- ½ orange pepper
- ½ yellow pepper
- 60g / 2oz sweet corn (½ cup)
- 60g / 2oz peas (½ cup)
- ½ courgette *

DRESSING:
- 30ml / 2 Tbsp red wine vinegar
- 90ml / 6 Tbsp olive oil
- 5ml / 1 tsp wholegrain mustard

- 5ml / 1 tsp honey
- 15ml / 1 Tbsp finely chopped parsley
- Salt and pepper to taste

FOR THE GARNISH:
- 55g / 2oz raw cashews (½ cup)
- 1 perfectly ripe mango
- 1 small avocado
- 10ml / 2 tsp fresh lemon juice
- A handful of cress or micro-greens
- A handful of edible flowers, such as nasturtiums

* Refer to glossary

I use Bulgur wheat combined with red and white quinoa for the salad in this recipe, but you can also use any combination of basmati, jasmine, brown, wild or camargue red rice (especially if you are cooking for someone with a wheat or gluten intolerance). I recommend mixing the chicken into the sauce the night before you serve this, as it allows the flavours to develop, and it becomes even more delicious!

"This is my interpretation of Coronation chicken, a dish that was created especially for Her Majesty The Queen's Coronation celebrations in June 1953. When I make this, it always brings back fond memories of the many buffet lunches that I prepared aboard HMY Britannia (the Royal Yacht)."

Method

Serves 4

1. Make the sauce: Simmer the curry powder and honey together in a small heavy-based saucepan for a few minutes, watching it closely as it catches and burns very easily.

2. Add the wine and chutney and cook for a further 3 minutes, then leave to cool.

3. When completely cold, stir the curry mixture into the mayonnaise. Whip the cream and then fold it into the curried mayonnaise.

4. Dice the chicken into 1cm (½ inch) cubes and mix it into the sauce. (If possible, leave the chicken overnight before serving.)

5. Make the mixed grain salad: Cook the grains according to the instructions. Drain and leave to cool.

6. Dice the peppers, cook the peas and sweet corn and grate the courgette. Toss all the vegetables into mixed grains.

7. Make the dressing by shaking all the ingredients together in a jar. Season to taste. Add the dressing to the mixed grain salad and mix well.

8. Lightly toast the cashews. Dice the mango. Slice the avocado and sprinkle with lemon juice.

9. Pile the chicken in the centre of a plate or dish and surround it with the mixed grain salad. Decorate with mango, avocado, cashews, cress and edible flowers.

T his is one of my favourite things to make, especially with my two very small helpers, aged 2 and 6, both of whom love rolling and cutting the gnocchi and, most of all, eating them! Once you have eaten these tender hearted nuggets with a crispy outside, you will never again want to eat commercially made gnocchi. I use basil, parsley and chives in this recipe, but you can use whatever combination of soft fresh herbs is available to you.

Fresh Herb Gnocchi
WITH TOMATO, BASIL AND MOZZARELLA

Ingredients

FOR THE GNOCCHI:
- 500g / 1lb 2oz floury potatoes (2 large baking potatoes)
- 1 free-range egg (UK medium / USA large) *
- 120g / 4oz plain flour * (1 cup)
- A generous handful each of fresh basil, parsley and chives
- Salt, pepper and nutmeg

FOR THE GARNISH:
- 8 plum tomatoes
- 60g / 2oz freshly grated parmesan (½ cup)
- 60ml / 4 Tbsp olive
- 20 bocconcini * OR 2 large balls of mozzarella cut into small pieces
- A generous handful of Greek basil leaves
- Salt and freshly ground black pepper

* Refer to glossary

Method

Makes 4 medium sized portions

1. To make the Gnocchi: Wash the potatoes, but do not peel them. Cook in boiling salted water until fork tender. Drain them and pop them on a baking tray in a low oven for about 10 minutes, to dry them out. Leave them to cool a little before peeling off the skins. Mash them with a fork, rub them through a sieve or put them through a vegetable mill.

2. Rinse and roughly chop the herbs.

3. Place the mashed potato in a large mixing bowl and add the egg, flour and all the herbs into a well in the centre. Bring it all together to form a smooth dough, that is neither sticky nor too dry; adding more flour if necessary, use either your hands or a spoon. Season with salt, pepper and nutmeg.

4. On a well-floured board, roll the dough into long thin sausage shapes about 1cm (½ inch). Chill for at least 15 minutes, then cut them into small 3cm (1¼ inch) chunks.

5. Place them on a floured tray. (If not using immediately, then freeze them. They can be cooked very successfully from frozen.)

6. To cook the gnocchi: Place them into a large pan of simmering water with salt and a splash of oil. When they rise to the surface, they are cooked; this takes 1 – 2 minutes depending on their size. Drain well.

7. Peel, seed and dice the plum tomatoes. Keep on one side.

8. Heat 2 tablespoons of olive oil in a non-stick frying pan. Toss the gnocchi into the pan to crisp them up, when they are crisp and golden in colour add the tomato fillets to warm them through.

9. Pile the gnocchi and tomato fillets onto warmed plates. Toss a few bocconcini (or some diced mozzarella) onto each plate, sprinkle with grated parmesan and small sprigs of Greek basil. Drizzle with the remaining olive oil and finish with a few twists of black pepper. Serve immediately.

MEMORANDUM
From
H.R.H. The Prince of Wales

May 20th 19 89.

To Carolyn

The note I received from HRH The Prince of Wales when I cooked a 'trial' dinner for Their Royal Highnesses at Highgrove. I got the job!

Fritatta Of New Potatoes
WITH PEAS, PARMESAN AND PANCETTA

P otatoes, peas, parmesan and pancetta; this is such a delectable combination. I would happily eat this frittata hot or cold, at a table or on a mountain top, for breakfast, lunch or supper. However, the best frittatas are often the 'spontaneous' ones; made from fresh vegetables from your garden or left-overs in your refrigerator, particularly small left-over ends of cheese.

Ingredients

YOU WILL NEED:
One 20cm (8 inch) heavy-based, oven-proof frying pan, preferably non-stick

- 8 spring onions *
- 170g / 6oz fresh or frozen peas (1½ cups)
- 120g / 4oz fresh spinach
- 24 small new potatoes (350g / 12oz)
- 30g / 2 Tbsp butter
- 30ml / 2 Tbsp olive oil
- 30ml / 2 Tbsp chopped chives, basil and parsley
- 50g / 2oz finely grated parmesan (½ cup)
- 10 free-range eggs (UK medium / USA large) *
- 175ml / ¾ cup double cream *
- Salt, pepper and nutmeg
- 120g / 4oz feta cheese, crumbled (1 cup)
- 15 thin slices pancetta (100g / 3½oz)

* Refer to glossary

Method

Makes one 20cm (8 inch) Frittata
Serves 6 – for breakfast, lunch or supper

1. Wash the spring onions and cut them into 5cm (2inch) lengths.

2. Cook the peas, keep on one side.

3. Wash the spinach, drain it well and wilt it in a little olive oil in a frying pan, keep on one side.

4. Cook the new potatoes until tender, drain and keep on one side.

5. Melt the butter with the olive oil in the pan in which you will cook the frittata. Cook the spring onions until they are soft. Remove the pan from the heat then add the peas, wilted spinach and potatoes. Sprinkle with the fresh herbs and parmesan.

6. Whisk together the eggs and cream and season with salt, pepper and nutmeg and pour it over the vegetables.

7. Crumble the feta cheese over and lastly add the pancetta in small twists. You can 'stir it up' a little with a fork so that you can see some of the ingredients on the top and you get the lovely green of the spinach to contrast with the white feta cheese and the pink pancetta.

8. Bake at 180ºC / 350ºF for 20 – 30 minutes, until it is set and the top is golden.

9. This is delicious eaten straight from the oven. Serve with a salad of mixed leaves with a balsamic dressing and warm crusty bread.

Crunchy Parmesan-Crusted Chicken
WITH ASPARAGUS AND LEMON PAPPARDELLE

T his is quick to prepare, and the fresh flavours of citrus and asparagus are beautifully summery. Vegetarians love the asparagus pappardelle on its own, without the chicken. Alternatively, the chicken is delicious served with avocado, mixed leaves and a lemon and olive oil dressing instead of the pasta. So you get three dishes for the price of one with this recipe!

Ingredients

- 4 free-range chicken breasts (140g / 5oz each)
- 30g / 1oz butter (2 Tbsp)

FOR THE PARMESAN CRUST:
- 40g / 1½oz butter (3 Tbsp)
- 85g / 3oz fresh breadcrumbs (1 cup)
- 60g / 2oz freshly grated parmesan (½ cup)
- 15ml / 1 Tbsp mixed fresh thyme leaves, parsley and marjoram, finely chopped
- A few twists of freshly ground black pepper
- 5ml / 1 tsp finely grated lemon zest

FOR THE PASTA:
- 16 asparagus spears
- 200g / 7oz pappardelle pasta
- 150ml / ⅔ cup crème fraîche
- 60g / 2oz pine nuts * (½ cup)
- 60g / 2oz wild rocket *
- Zest of 1 lemon
- A few parmesan shavings

* Refer to glossary

Method

Serves 4

1. Preheat the oven to 190ºC / 375ºF.

2. To make the parmesan crust, melt the butter and combine it with all the other ingredients and mix well.

3. Remove the skin from the chicken. Melt the butter in a sauté pan and sear the chicken, so that each side is lightly golden in colour; 2 -3 minutes on each side, then place it on a baking tray. Divide the topping between the four breasts, 'packing' it down well so that it doesn't fall off during cooking.

4. Bake in the oven for 20 – 25 minutes, until the topping is crisp and golden and the chicken is cooked through.

5. Meanwhile prepare the asparagus. Trim off the woody section at the base of each stem and cut the remainder into 2.5cm (1 inch) lengths. Cook in salted boiling water until tender.

6. Cook the pappardelle in boiling salted water, according to the instructions, drain it and return it to the pan.

7. Simmer the crème fraîche gently in a small pan for a couple of minutes then stir it into the pappardelle with the asparagus, pine nuts and rocket. Grate the lemon zest onto the pasta and finish with freshly ground black pepper.

8. Serve the pasta immediately in a warm serving dish or directly onto warm plates. Top with the chicken breasts and parmesan shavings.

Herb–Baked Seabass,

CARAMELISED FENNEL, VINE TOMATOES AND SPINACH WITH LEMON-HERB BUTTER

The flavour of seabass is delicate and is easily smothered by rich, creamy sauces or strong flavours, which is why I just use a simple citrus butter with herbs to keep the fish moist whilst baking it. I serve the fish with spinach, fennel and tomatoes, which bring colour to the plate and a diversity of flavours to the palate, but which still allow the flavour of the Seabass to shine through. My father always enjoyed eating fish and I loved preparing this dish for him, using his own home-grown spinach and tomatoes.

Ingredients

FOR THE HERB BUTTER:

- 85g / 3oz butter (6 Tbsp)
- A handful each of fresh dill and flat-leaf parsley
- A pinch of salt
- A twist of freshly ground black pepper
- Zest of 1 lemon
- 10ml / 2 tsp fresh lemon juice

- 4 fillets of seabass, skin on (140g / 5oz each)
- 60ml / 4 Tbsp olive oil
- 1 stem of mini vine tomatoes, (about 20 tomatoes)
- salt, pepper and a touch of sugar
- 4 bulbs of fennel
- 400g (14oz) baby spinach

My father, still tending his vegetables, aged 87. Here he is picking some spinach, 'assisted' by his beloved cat, Sam.

Method

Serves 4

1. Preheat the oven to 180ºC / 350ºF

2. Prepare the fennel by removing the very coarse outer layer and trimming the base. Cut each bulb in half or into quarters, depending on how big they are. Heat the olive oil in a heavy-based frying pan and add the fennel, cook over a high heat for a few minutes, turning it over several times to brown it on all sides. Then cover with lid or some aluminium foil and leave to cook more slowly for a further 15 – 20 minutes, until it is soft.

3. Rinse the herbs if necessary and dry before chopping them finely. Make the herb butter by combining all the ingredients and beating with a hand-held electric mixer until it is light and fluffy.

4. Make the herb butter by combining all the ingredients and beating with a hand-held electric mixer until it is light and fluffy.

5. Lay the seabass fillets skin-side down on a baking tray with a little olive oil on it. Spread a little of the herb butter (reserving some for the garnish) on each piece of fish, season lightly with salt and freshly ground black pepper and cover the baking tray with foil. Bake for 12 – 15 minutes.

6. Bake the tomatoes at the same time as the fish, but on a separate baking tray. They should be pricked with a fork, seasoned with salt, pepper and sugar and drizzled with a little olive oil before cooking.

7. Wilt the spinach in a frying pan with a little of the lemon herb butter, season and drain off any excess liquid.

8. To serve: Divide the spinach between the four plates and top with a piece of seabass. Garnish with a few little tomatoes and several pieces of the caramelised fennel. Finish with a little more of the green herb butter on the fish.

ooking with salmon brings back fond memories of my many trips to Balmoral, in Scotland, with HRH The Prince of Wales. We were always there in the months between February and September (the salmon fishing season on the river Dee). If His Royal Highness was going fishing and I suggested salmon as an option on the menu, the answer always came back, 'Only if I catch one!' It was prudent to have something else on standby, just in case the fishing party arrived home empty handed.

Seared Salmon Fillet

SERVED ON A BLACK BEAN, TOMATO & AVOCADO SALSA

Ingredients

FOR THE SALSA:

- 120g / 4oz dried black beans (½ cup)
  NOTE: these need to be soaked overnight before use
- Sea salt and freshly ground black pepper
- 45ml / 3 Tbsp of virgin olive oil
- 25ml / 1½ Tbsp of lime juice
- 1 small red onion
- 2 large ripe plum tomatoes
- 1 medium avocado, ripe but firm
- A good handful of Greek basil leaves
- A handful of wild rocket *

FOR THE SALMON:

- 4 pieces skinned salmon fillet
  (170g / 6oz each)
- 30ml / 2 Tbsp mild olive oil
- Finely grated zest of 1 orange
- Finely grated zest of 2 limes
- Freshly ground black pepper
- A little olive oil for cooking the salmon

* Refer to glossary

Method

Serves 4

1. Soak the beans overnight, rinse them thoroughly and place them in a saucepan, cover with cold water and bring to the boil. Simmer for approximately 40 minutes, until tender (according to the specific instructions for the beans you are using). Drain, rinse under cold water and then place them in a large bowl. Season the beans with sea salt and freshly ground black pepper. Mix in the olive oil and lime juice. Finely dice the onion and add it to the beans. Cover and leave for about an hour for the flavours to develop. (Don't be tempted to use tinned black beans – you will be disappointed in the flavour and appearance of the beans and especially the mushy texture.)

2. Before you cook the salmon, brush each piece of fish with a little olive oil, grate the orange and lime zest directly onto it (you will lose all the wonderful aromatic essential oils from the citrus if you grate the zest onto a plate and then transfer it to the fish). Grind some black pepper over it then turn the fish over and repeat the process. Cover with plastic wrap and chill for 20 minutes before cooking.

3. While the salmon is resting, skin, seed and dice the tomatoes and also dice the avocado in 5mm (¼ inch) cubes.

4. Mix the diced tomato and avocado into the beans with the basil and rocket. Check the seasoning and add more salt and pepper if required.

5. To cook the salmon: Preheat a heavy-based frying pan (preferably non-stick) with a little olive oil.

6. When the pan is hot, add the pieces of salmon fillet and cook for 2 – 3 minutes on each side, according to the thickness of the fish. The fish should become a little crisp on the outside.

7. To serve, pile some of the salsa into the centre of a plate and place the warm salmon on top.

Simple Roast Fillet Of Beef

WITH CELERIAC, GREEN BEANS AND ARTICHOKES AND A MUSHROOM CREAM SAUCE

Ingredients

- 4 small globe artichokes
- 1 lemon
- A little olive oil
- 150g / 5½oz green beans
- 400g / 14oz celeriac * (1 large root)
- 120g / 4oz butter (8 Tbsp)
- 4 fillet steaks * (185g / 6oz each)
- 100g / 3½oz fresh porcini mushrooms *
- 100g / 3½oz fresh chestnut mushrooms *
- A few sprigs of fresh thyme
- 150ml / ⅔ cup double cream *
- Salt and freshly ground black pepper

* Refer to glossary

Method

Serves 4

1. Prepare the artichokes: Fill a bowl with cold water and squeeze the juice of half a lemon into it. Snap the stem off each artichoke and then pull off the outer leaves, until you reach the cream/purple inner leaves. Using a small, sharp knife trim away the small inner leaves and peel around the base of the artichoke heart, for a neat circular shape. Turn the heart on its side and using a large chef's knife, cut straight across the top of the heart removing the spiky choke. Use a teaspoon to scrape off the remaining 'hairs' from the centre of the heart. Drop each artichoke into the lemon water as soon as it is prepared, to prevent it from discolouring. Cook them until tender, in boiling salted water with a few slivers of lemon and a trickle of olive oil. They will take 10 – 12 minutes.

2. Top and tail the green beans, wash and cook in boiling lightly salted water until they are tender. Refresh in iced water and keep on one side.

3. Peel the celeriac, then using a large sharp knife, cut it into very thin slivers. Melt 60g (4 tablespoons) of the butter in a large, preferably non-stick, frying pan and cook the celeriac until it is very tender and golden around the edges.

4. Melt 30g (2 tablespoons) of the butter and brush it onto the steaks, season them with salt and pepper. Heat a non-stick frying pan and cook them for 4 – 5 minutes, turning them to seal them on all sides. Transfer the steaks to a baking tray and cook them at 220ºC / 425ºF for a further 8 – 10 minutes, for a medium-cooked steak.

5. While the steak is in the oven, clean and slice the mushrooms. Sauté them in the remaining butter, using the frying pan that the steak was cooked in. Season with salt and pepper, add the thyme and the cream and cook the sauce for a couple of minutes to reduce it slightly.

6. To serve: Reheat the beans, artichoke hearts and celeriac in a little olive oil. Place the celeriac on warmed plates with the steak on top. Surround with the beans and artichokes. Spoon the mushroom sauce over the steaks and serve immediately.

*P*reparing the artichokes for this dish will take time and some skill (and will also leave you with stained hands) but it's worth all the effort. However, if time is of the essence, or fresh artichokes are not available, then you can use the small artichokes in oil that you find in most Italian delicatessens.

Spring Lamb Salad

L amb was a great favourite of HRH The Princess of Wales, especially when it was served with plenty of mint. This salad is quick to prepare and the lime and mint vinaigrette is deliciously tangy.

Ingredients

FOR THE MINT VINAIGRETTE:

- 1 small shallot
- 30ml / 2 Tbsp lime juice
- 15ml / 1 Tbsp white wine vinegar
- 2.5ml / ½ tsp Dijon mustard
- 90ml / 6 Tbsp mild olive oil or grape seed oil
- Salt, pepper and brown sugar
- 30ml / 2 Tbsp finely chopped mint
- 15ml / 1 Tbsp finely chopped parsley

FOR THE LAMB SALAD:

- 1 fully boned and trimmed rack of lamb
- A splash of olive oil
- 100g / 3½oz mixed salad leaves
- ¼ cucumber
- 12 mini plum tomatoes *
- 12 Kalamata olives
- ½ red onion
- 200g / 7oz feta cheese, crumbled (1¾ cup)
- A handful of fresh mint leaves

* Refer to glossary

Method

Serves 4

1. Make the vinaigrette: Finely chop the shallot and place it in a large bowl or jug with the lime juice, vinegar and mustard. Blend together using either a balloon whisk or a handheld stick blender. Add the oil in a slow stream, allowing the vinaigrette to emulsify and thicken. Season to taste with salt, pepper and a pinch of brown sugar.

2. You can prepare the vinaigrette in advance to this stage. The mint and parsley should be added just before the dish is served as they lose their lovely bright green colour very quickly.

3. Heat a heavy-based frying pan or skillet over a high heat then add the olive oil. Season the lamb with salt and pepper and add it to the pan. Sear well until it is browned on all sides and medium rare inside, about 8 – 10 minutes. Cover to keep it warm and leave to rest for 10 minutes before slicing it.

4. Blend the herbs into the vinaigrette. Slice the cucumber and red onion very thinly.

5. In a large bowl toss all the salad ingredients, with a little of the vinaigrette. Arrange the salad in a mound on a serving dish and top with the slices of lamb.

6. Finish by drizzling some of the vinaigrette over the lamb. Serve immediately.

Carolyn.

Wishing you a very Happy Christmas
and New Year
1993

from. Diana.

*A Christmas Card from Diana,
HRH The Princess of Wales*

Summer Ratatouille
WITH SEARED TUNA

I spent two fantastic weeks in Provence, working alongside the brilliant chef, Roger Vergé, in his Michelin-starred restaurant, Le Moulin de Mougins. I was sent to France by His Royal Highness, to learn some of the secrets of Provencal cuisine, first hand. It was an incredible opportunity and a dream come true for me to meet and work alongside Monsieur Vergé, whom I greatly admire and respect. The fresh, local produce used in the restaurant was magnificent; plump glossy aubergines, beautiful courgette blossoms, amazingly aromatic tomatoes, vividly coloured sweet peppers and, of course, there was garlic aplenty. This dish makes me think of that astonishing, sunny, colourful cuisine that so inspired me. For a vegetarian meal replace the tuna in this recipe with baked goats' cheese and serve with some chunky sourdough croutons.

Ingredients

- 4 tuna steaks (150g / 5oz each)

FOR THE RATATOUILLE:
- 8 mini courgettes *
- 8 mini aubergines *
- 6 plum tomatoes

- 2 sweet yellow peppers
- 2 sweet red peppers
- A good handful of fresh Greek basil
- Olive oil
- Balsamic vinegar
- Salt and black pepper

* Refer to glossary

Method

Serves 4

1. Preheat the oven to 200ºC / 400ºF.

2. Cut the courgettes, aubergines and tomatoes in half lengthwise. Halve the peppers and de-seed them. Place all the vegetables in a large bowl. Drizzle with olive oil and balsamic vinegar and season with salt and freshly ground black pepper and toss them. Turn them into a large roasting tin, and cook for 20 – 30 minutes, turning them several times during cooking, until they are soft and lightly coloured.

3. Heat a little olive oil in a heavy-based frying pan. Season the tuna and sear it, turning as needed, until it is just coloured on all sides. This will take 3-5 minutes.

4. Leave to stand for a couple of minutes.

5. Pile the warm roasted vegetables onto a serving dish or individual plates. Place the tuna on top.

6. Sprinkle with plenty of Greek basil, and drizzle with extra olive oil and balsamic vinegar. Finish with a few twists of freshly ground black pepper. Serve immediately.

A piece from the local newspaper about my time at Le Moulins de Mougins

Warm & Comforting

MAIN COURSES FOR THE WINTER

Aubergine, Tomato
AND GOATS' CHEESE STACK

Although this is a vegetarian dish, it is always happily devoured by non-vegetarians alike. It is hearty yet healthy. It is satisfying yet it is still a light meal. Served with a crispy baked potato and extra tomato sauce and parmesan, it is a warming meal for the winter. When served with a simple salad and some crusty bread, it is perfect for the summer. This is one of many variations that I have made over the years. It is a dish that I regularly made for HRH The Princess of Wales.

(The quantity of tomato sauce that I make in this recipe allows for some extra to serve with the aubergine.)

Ingredients

- 2 large aubergines *
- Olive oil, salt & freshly ground black pepper
- 1 yellow pepper
- 1 red pepper
- 1 red onion
- 100g / 3½oz bulgur wheat
- 1 sprig of fresh thyme
- 150g / 5½oz goats' cheese log
- 60g / 2oz finely grated parmesan (½ cup)
- A handful of fresh basil leaves

FOR THE TOMATO SAUCE:

- 2 onions
- 2 cloves of garlic
- A little olive oil
- 800g / 1lb 12oz tin * of plum tomatoes
- 2 sprigs of fresh thyme
- Salt, black pepper and sugar

* Refer to glossary

Method

Serves 4

1. Preheat the oven to 200ºC / 400ºF.

2. Wash the aubergines and cut them in half length-wise. Score the flesh with a sharp knife, season with salt and freshly ground black pepper and drizzle with olive oil.

3. Bake the aubergines for about 30 minutes, or until the flesh is soft.

4. While the aubergine is baking, make the tomato sauce: Finely dice the onion and crush the garlic, then sauté them together in the olive oil until the onion is soft and translucent. Add the tomatoes and thyme and season with salt, pepper and sugar to taste. Cook slowly with the lid on for 30 minutes, then for a further 15 minutes with the lid off, to allow some of the liquid to evaporate so that the sauce thickens.

5. Dice the peppers and sauté them in a little olive oil, until they are soft. Keep on one side.

6. Finely chop the red onion and sauté it in a little olive oil, add the bulgur wheat and some water, as per the specific cooking instructions of the bulgur wheat you are using. It generally it cooks in about 12 minutes but check this as it varies with different brands.

7. Once the aubergine is ready, scrape the flesh out carefully, so as not to damage the skins. Chop the flesh and mix in the fresh thyme leaves. Season to taste with salt and pepper. Return the skins to the baking tray ready to fill.

Continued ⇥

Method Continued

8. Begin with a layer of bulgur wheat in the base of the aubergine skin.

9. Slice the goats' cheese log into 12 rounds and then halve them into semi-circles. Place 3 pieces into each aubergine.

10. Next, add a layer of aubergine flesh.

11. Cover this with some tomato sauce.

12. Sprinkle a generous layer of grated parmesan onto the sauce.

13. Now another layer of bulgur wheat.

14. Top this with the diced sautéed peppers and more grated parmesan.

15. Finish with a generous covering of tomato sauce and a few more pieces of goats' cheese.

16. Bake at 200ºC / 400ºF for 25 minutes.

17. Just before serving, toss a few little basil leaves on top and accompany the aubergine with the remaining tomato sauce and some extra grated parmesan.

Variations

• If you serve this with a baked potato, new potatoes or some crusty bread and a green salad it makes a lovely vegetarian main course.

• If you replace the bulgur wheat with quinoa or rice, then this is perfect for anyone with a gluten or wheat intolerance.

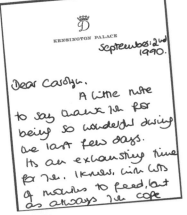

A lovely note from HRH The Princess of Wales after a busy weekend

"*Although this is a vegetarian dish, it is always happily devoured by non-vegetarians alike...*"

Farro With Winter Vegetables,
HERBS AND POACHED CHICKEN

Farro originates in Tuscany, it is a brown grain with a delightfully nutty taste and firm texture. It is similar to pearl barley but cooks much more quickly. This is half way between being a soup and a casserole - either way, it is very hearty, warming winter fare. It is a really versatile recipe, you can use any combination of vegetables - whatever is growing in your garden or looks good at the Farmers' market! It is also a great way to use up left over roast chicken, which saves you having to buy chicken breasts.

I have included this recipe in the book for my late husband Bill Hootkins, who regarded chicken soup as the cure for all ills; although when he made it, he put so many chilli peppers in it, that it was either kill or cure!

Ingredients

- 2 large shallots
- 18 baby carrots
- 150g / 5½oz waxy potatoes *
- 200g / 7oz butternut
- 2 sticks of celery
- 1 leek
- 30ml / 2 Tbsp mild olive oil
- 30g / 1oz butter (2 Tbsp)
- A few sprigs of fresh thyme
- 150ml / ½ cup white wine
- 600ml / 2 cups chicken stock *
- 2 chicken breasts (Approx 150g / 5oz each)
- 100g / 3½oz farro (½ cup)
- 12 small florets of broccoli

* Refer to glossary

Method

Makes 6 hearty portions

1. Finely dice the shallots. Top and tail the baby carrots and wash them, but you don't need to peel them. Dice the potatoes and butternut into small 1cm (½ inch) cubes. Wash, de-string and slice the celery and chop the leek into thin rings and rinse well.

2. Heat the olive oil and butter in a large heavy-based saucepan. Sauté all the vegetables over a high heat for several minutes, stirring well to coat everything in butter. Add the sprigs of thyme.

3. Cover and cook over a medium heat for about 10 minutes, to soften the vegetables. Add the white wine, stock and chicken breasts and cook slowly with the lid on for a further 20 minutes. Remove the chicken and leave it to cool.

4. Add the farro and simmer for 12 – 15 minutes, until it is tender. While this is cooking, dice the chicken.

5. Return the chicken to the pan, add the broccoli and cook everything together slowly for a further 10 minutes. (I add the broccoli right at the end so that it maintains a little 'crunch' and keeps its bright green colour.)

6. Serve into warmed soup bowls, accompanied by freshly baked Soda Bread (see recipe on page 220) for a wholesome winter's feast.

My Tip

If you can make this the day before you need it, the flavours will develop and it will be even more delicious.

The buckwheat flour in these crêpes imparts a deliciously earthy flavour to this dish. The combination of spinach, leeks and bacon with cheese and cream is one that I come back to time and again. Topped with a poached egg, these crêpes would be sure to get the royal seal of approval.

This quantity of batter makes about twelve crêpes, which is more than you need for this recipe. The batter keeps in the refrigerator for 24 hours, so you don't have to make and eat them all on the same day. (They are also delicious rolled up with lemon and sugar or with chocolate spread inside!)

Buckwheat Crêpes

WITH SPINACH, LEEKS, BACON AND GRUYÈRE CHEESE

Ingredients

YOU WILL NEED:

1 non-stick pan suitable for making crêpes, about 20cm (8inch) diameter. One ovenproof dish, approximately 22cm (9 inches) square

FOR THE CRÊPE BATTER:

- 75g / 1¾oz plain flour * (⅔ cup)
- 75g / 1¾oz buckwheat flour (⅔ cup)
- A pinch of salt
- 2 free-range eggs (UK medium / USA large) *
- 110ml / ½ cup water
- 225ml / 1 cup whole milk
- 15ml / 1 Tbsp oil

FOR THE FILLING AND TOPPING:

- 120g / 4oz streaky bacon (4 rashers)
- 4 leeks
- 30g / 1oz butter (2 Tbsp)
- 250g / 9oz spinach
- 200ml / ¾ cup whipping cream *
- 120g / 4oz cave-aged gruyère cheese
- Salt, black pepper and nutmeg

* Refer to glossary

Method

Makes 2 hearty portions

1. Make the batter: Sift the flours and a large pinch of salt into a medium bowl and make a well in the centre. Using a whisk gradually beat in the eggs and 110ml (½ cup) of water to make a smooth batter.

2. Whisk in the milk, then cover and chill for at least 2 hours. This allows the batter to thicken, making soft, delicately textured pancakes. The batter can also be left overnight.

3. For the filling, dice the bacon and then fry it until crispy. Wash and dice the leeks then cook them in butter in the same pan as you used for bacon, until they are soft.

4. Wash the spinach, drain it, cook it lightly in a little olive oil and squeeze out any excess liquid. Mix the spinach with the bacon and leeks, keep on one side.

5. Bring the cream to a rolling boil, season to taste with nutmeg, salt and pepper.

6. Preheat the oven to 200ºC / 400ºF.

7. Make the pancakes: Heat 1 teaspoon of oil in a non-stick pan, then soak up any excess with a piece of kitchen paper. Add just enough batter to the hot pan to cover the surface when swirled, cook for 30 – 40 seconds and then flip over by sliding a spatula underneath and cook for a further 30 – 40 seconds on the other side. Repeat the process until you have 4 perfect pancakes.

8. Divide the filling evenly between the pancakes and lay them, open-faced in a buttered oven-proof dish. Pour the warm cream over the pancakes and sprinkle with the grated gruyère cheese.

9. Place the dish on a baking tray and bake for 20 – 25 minutes, until golden and bubbling.

Creamed Chicken

WITH MORELS, BACON AND SHALLOTS SERVED WITH CAMARGUE RED RICE

*T*his simple dish is quick to prepare and the chicken is always wonderfully succulent and tender. The combination of flavours – morels, smoked bacon, white wine and thyme – is heavenly! You can serve this dish with any rice, but I find the colour and flavour of Camargue red rice so much more interesting than most other varieties. Dried morels are not always readily available, but do try to find some, it is definitely worth the effort. They have a more concentrated flavour than the fresh ones and contribute a rich, wonderful taste to any dish. (Fine grit can hide in the tiny crevices in a morel, so be sure to rinse them thoroughly when you soak them in water to reconstitute them.)

Ingredients

- 30g / 1oz large dried morels
- 150g / 5½oz smoked streaky bacon (about 6 slices)
- 6 shallots
- 2 cloves garlic
- 30ml / 2 Tbsp olive oil
- 30g / 1oz butter (2 Tbsp)
- 4 chicken breasts (skin on)
- A few sprigs of fresh thyme
- 225ml / 1 cup dry white wine
- 150ml / ⅔ cup double cream *
- Salt and freshly ground black pepper
- 225g / 8oz Camargue Red rice (uncooked weight)

* Refer to glossary

Method

Serves 4

1. Soak the dried morels in cold water for about 20 minutes to reconstitute them. Rinse thoroughly and dry them on kitchen paper.

2. Dice the bacon and the shallots roughly & crush the garlic.

3. In a heavy-based casserole pan, such as 'Le Creuset', heat the oil and add the bacon, fry until crisp, then set aside. In the same pan, fry the shallots and garlic until golden, then set aside. Lastly, cook the morels in butter for a couple of minutes then remove them from the pan.

4. Return pan to the heat and sear the chicken breasts on both sides over a high heat. The skin should be very crisp and a rich golden colour.

5. Return the bacon, shallots, garlic and morels to the casserole pan with the chicken. Add the sprigs of fresh thyme and pour in the white wine and cream.

6. Bring to a very gentle simmer and cook slowly for 20 minutes with the lid on.

7. Leave to stand for 10 minutes. Check the seasoning and add more salt or pepper if necessary.

8. Serve with Camargue red rice (cooked as per the instructions on the packet).

Smoked Haddock Kedgeree

WITH SHREDDED LEEKS, CREAMED SPINACH AND QUAILS' EGGS

Traditionally, kedgeree is a breakfast dish, however, presented like this it makes an appealing supper dish, which is perfect for eating on your lap in front of a roaring log fire. If you have left-over poached salmon, flake it and use it instead of the smoked haddock, which is not always readily available. Salmon tastes delicious and the pink colour looks attractive with the green spinach and leeks. If quails' eggs are unavailable you can use a small regular egg either soft boiled or poached.

Ingredients

- 300g / 10oz smoked haddock *
- 1 medium onion
- 2 leeks
- 90g / 3oz butter (6 Tbsp)
- 5ml / 1 tsp curry powder
- 170g / 6oz basmati rice (1 cup)
- A good pinch of saffron
- 150g / 5oz baby spinach
- 15ml / 1 Tbsp olive oil
- 120ml / ½ cup whipping cream *
- 2 free-range eggs, hard boiled and chopped (UK medium / USA large) *
- 15ml / 1 Tbsp finely chopped parsley
- 4 quails' eggs
- Freshly ground black pepper

* Refer to glossary

Method

Serves 4

1. Place the haddock fillets in a saucepan and cover with cold water, bring to a gentle simmer then turn down the heat. Put the lid on the saucepan and cook gently for 6 – 8 minutes, until the haddock is cooked through. Leave to cool.

2. Chop the onions finely and then the leeks, keeping the green and white portions separate.

3. Put the rice in a sieve and rinse well under cold running water. Leave to drain.

4. Melt 1oz (2 tablespoons) of the butter in a saucepan and sauté the onion and the white part of the leeks with the curry powder for a few minutes. Add the rinsed rice and the saffron and stir well. Cook for 2 minutes then add water to the pan and continue to cook (as per the cooking instructions on the packet).

5. While the rice is cooking, sauté the green portion of the leeks in 1oz (2 tablespoons) of the butter until they are tender. Keep on one side.

6. Wash and drain the spinach, then sauté it in a pan with a little olive oil. Squeeze out any excess liquid and mix with 60ml (4 tablespoons) of the cream.

7. Remove all skin and bones from the haddock and flake it. Add it to the cooked rice. Add the chopped boiled eggs and parsley.

8. Soft-boil 4 quails' eggs, and peel them. Keep them warm in hot water until required.

9. Heat the remaining cream and butter and stir this into the rice mixture.

10. Ensure that the kedgeree is thoroughly heated through then divide it between 4 buttered rings or ramekins. Reheat the green leeks and spinach. Divide the spinach between four warm plates. Turn out the kedgeree on to the spinach. Garnish the top of each one with the shredded green leeks and a warm quail's egg. Serve immediately.

Potato & Sage Torte
WITH LAMB AND APRICOT RAGOUT

Potato and sage torte – layer upon layer of finely slivered potato interspersed with meltingly soft buttery onions, sage leaves and cheddar cheese. Topped with golden, crispy potato... I have made this using many different varieties of potatoes and 'King Edwards' definitely give the best result.

Lamb and apricot ragout – slowly cooked, rich meat sauce with the subtle flavours of apricot and thyme. Cooked over a very low heat for 3 hours, the ragout has a velvety texture that is also perfect for a shepherd's pie or to serve with home-made herb gnocchi (see recipe on page 65)

Ingredients

YOU WILL NEED:

One 15 – 18cm (6 – 7 inch) non-stick deep spring-form tin

FOR THE LAMB & APRICOT RAGOUT:

- 400g / 14oz lamb mince *
- 1 large onion
- 1 large carrot
- 1 large leek
- 2 sticks of celery
- 1 clove of garlic, crushed
- A few sprigs of fresh thyme
- A little olive oil
- 400g / 14oz tin of chopped plum tomatoes *
- 10 soft dried apricots, diced
- 250ml / 1 cup water
- Salt and freshly ground black pepper

FOR THE POTATO & SAGE TORTE:

- 2 medium onions
- 750g / 1lb 11oz baking potatoes
- 110g / 4oz butter (1 stick)
- 50g / 2oz grated mature cheddar cheese (½ cup)
- 50g / 2oz grated parmesan (½ cup)
- A handful of fresh sage leaves
- Salt & freshly ground black pepper

* Refer to glossary

Method

Serves 6

1. Make the lamb ragout: Brown the lamb in a little olive oil in a heavy-based pan, then transfer it to a fine colander to drain off any excess fat.

2. Chop and sauté the vegetables with the crushed garlic in olive oil (in the pan you used for the lamb) over a high heat for a few minutes then return the meat to the pan and add the thyme, tinned tomatoes, dried apricots and water, stir well.

3. Bring to simmering point and then turn the heat right down so that the surface of the meat is barely moving. Cover with a lid and cook like this for 2½ hours. This very slow cooking produces a beautifully rich and thick ragout with a very soft texture. If at the end of this time the ragout still has quite a lot of liquid in it, cook it for a further 30 minutes with the lid off.

4. While the lamb is cooking, make the potato torte: Preheat the oven to 200ºC / 400ºF. Slice the onions very thinly. Peel and thinly slice the potatoes.

5. In a small heavy-based pan, fry the onions in 50g (4 tablespoons) of the butter. Cook slowly until golden and very soft. Season with salt and pepper.

Continued ⇢

"Potato and sage torte – layer upon layer of finely slivered potato interspersed with meltingly soft buttery onions, sage leaves and cheddar cheese. Topped with golden, crispy potato..."

Method Continued

6. Butter the spring-form tin, using some of the remaining butter.

7. Line the base of the tin with a layer of closely over-lapping potato slices. Do the same around the side of the tin. Spread about one fifth of the onion onto the base, sprinkle with a mixture of the two cheeses and several whole sage leaves. Top with another layer of potato, dot with a little more butter and season with salt and freshly ground black pepper.

8. Repeat these layers another 4 or 5 times, ending with a layer of potato and brush this with a little melted butter.

9. Place the tin on a baking tray and cover the top with some foil or baking parchment. Bake covered for 1 hour 20 minutes and then uncover and bake for a further 20 – 30 minutes to allow the top to crisp up. Allow to cool a little before removing from the tin; if you remove it from the tin too soon, it may collapse.

10. To serve, slice the potato torte into wedges and present it on a bed of ragout garnished with fresh herbs. Remember to remove the sprigs of thyme from the ragout before serving.

Variations

• The potato torte makes a delicious vegetarian main course, served with ratatouille and a green salad.

• You can make the torte using a selection of root vegetables such as carrots, parsnips and celeriac and you can vary the herbs – chives and thyme work really well.

• The lamb and apricot ragout is always popular with children, I think they like the sweetness of the apricots in it. I often serve it with small wedges of crispy polenta.

• Although not quite traditional, the ragout makes wonderful Moussaka - layer it up with sliced potato and roasted aubergine and top it with a layer of Greek yoghurt mixed with ricotta, parmesan and eggs.

Any chapter on 'warm and comforting' food would be incomplete without a recipe for a beef casserole; that most robust and hearty of all winter dishes. When braising meat, there are a few simple guidelines that I always adhere to. Firstly, do invest in a heavy duty, stovetop-to-oven casserole pan; I swear by my big old 'Le Creuset', which always gives good results. Always brown the diced meat very well before adding the wine. Use a decent red wine; Burgundy is my favourite with beef. Be generous in your use of hardy fresh herbs such as (thyme, rosemary and bay leaves); use whole sprigs and remove them just before serving - they lend a wonderful depth of flavour to the dish. Most importantly, never rush the cooking process.

Braised Beef With Red Wine,

PUYS LENTILS AND THYME,
SERVED WITH CREAMED CELERIAC

Ingredients

FOR THE BRAISED BEEF:

- 1kg / 2lb 4oz beef, in chunky 50g / 2oz cubes
- 45ml / 3 Tbsp plain flour *
- 30ml / 2 Tbsp oil
- 30g / 2 Tbsp butter
- 2 medium red onions
- 3 medium carrots
- 4 sticks celery
- 2 cloves garlic
- 750ml / 3 cups red wine
- 250ml / 1 cup water
- 85g / 3oz lentils
- 2.5ml / ½ tsp ground nutmeg
- 15ml / 1 Tbsp muscovado sugar *
- Several sprigs of fresh rosemary and thyme
- 24 small shallots

FOR THE CELERIAC MASH:

- 30g / 2 Tbsp butter
- 500g / 1lb 2oz celeriac * / one large celery root, peeled and diced
- A sprig each of thyme & rosemary
- Salt, black pepper and nutmeg

* Refer to glossary

Method

Serves 6

1. Preheat the oven to 150ºC / 300ºF.

2. Toss the beef in a large bowl with the flour, seasoned with salt and freshly ground black pepper.

3. Heat the oil and butter in a large heavy stovetop-to-oven casserole pan. Brown the diced beef in several batches, browning it all over, then transfer it to a bowl.

4. Chop the onions, carrots and celery and crush the garlic then sautè them, in the same pan as you used for the beef, until lightly browned.

5. Return the beef to the pan and add the red wine, water, lentils, nutmeg, sugar and herbs. Bring to a gentle simmer, then cover the surface with a piece of baking parchment, put the lid on and place in the oven for 90 minutes. Check several times during cooking.

6. Add the shallots and then return to the oven for a further 90 minutes.

7. While the casserole continues to cook, make the celeriac mash: Melt the butter in a medium saucepan add the diced celeriac, herbs and seasoning.

8. Cook with the lid on for about 30 minutes, stirring from time to time, until the celeriac is soft enough to purée. It should not need any extra liquid to be added, but keep a close eye on it, adding some if necessary.

9. Leave to cool a little before puréeing with a liquidiser or stick blender.

10. If at the end of cooking time, the sauce in the casserole looks 'watery', remove the meat and vegetables with a slotted spoon and boil the sauce to reduce it. You can also thicken it with a couple of teaspoons of flour mixed with butter or corn flour mixed with water, cook well after adding the thickening.

Baked Tortiglione
WITH THREE CHEESES,
VINE TOMATOES AND HERBS

*S*erve this for a quick lunch, a simple supper or even for a picnic. To transport it, wrap it in foil and tie it in a tea-towel and it will stay warm for a surprisingly long time. Instead of making cheese sauce, I save time by stirring crème fraîche through the pasta. I add diced gruyère cheese, which when baked gives little nuggets of molten cheese. The tiny oven-baked tomatoes contribute fantastic little explosions of piquancy to the dish.

Ingredients

- 225g / 8oz mini plum tomatoes *
- 4 sprigs of fresh thyme
- A splash of olive oil & balsamic vinegar
- Salt, black pepper and sugar
- 225g / 8oz tortiglioni pasta
- 300ml / 1¼ cups crème fraîche
- 150g / 5oz ricotta (¾ cup)
- 100g / 3½oz gruyère cheese (1 cup)
- 60g / 2oz finely grated parmesan (½ cup)
- Fresh basil and chives

* Refer to glossary

Method

Serves 4

1. Preheat the oven to 150ºC / 300ºF.

2. Wash the tomatoes and prick each one with a fork. Place on a small non-stick baking tray with the thyme. Drizzle with a little olive oil and balsamic vinegar, sprinkle with salt, pepper and a pinch of sugar. Roll them around to coat each one.

3. Bake for 45 - 60 minutes, until they look slightly 'shrivelled'.

4. When the tomatoes are ready, cook the pasta, as per the instructions on the packet and drain it.

5. Stir the crème fraîche through the pasta and layer it in a buttered oven-proof dish with the tomatoes, herbs, spoonfuls of ricotta, cubes of Gruyere and the grated parmesan cheese.

6. Place the dish on a baking tray and bake at 200ºC / 400ºF for 25 minutes.

7. Sprinkle with fresh herbs before serving.

Warm Salad

OF JERUSALEM ARTICHOKES WITH SMOKED BACON AND LEMON-PARSLEY DRESSING

Even for the most devoted of salad-eaters, a bowl of lettuce leaves loses its appeal in the depths of winter. This may not, strictly speaking, be a 'salad' but it is a deliciously light, yet still warming meal that always gets rave reviews. It has the robust flavour and crispness of the smoky bacon paired with the tang of the lemon-parsley dressing and the sweetness of the artichokes – so simple, yet stunning. I like to serve this with soda bread, fresh from the oven. Start to finish, you can have this on the table in just 30 minutes.

Ingredients

- 500g / 1lb 2oz Jerusalem artichokes
- 15 ml / 1 Tbsp lemon juice
- 200g / 7oz thinly sliced smoked streaky bacon (7-8 rashers *)
- 30g / 1oz butter (2 Tbsp)
- Salt and freshly ground black pepper

FOR THE DRESSING:
- Zest of 1 lemon
- 10ml / 2 tsp wholegrain mustard
- 5ml / 1 tsp honey
- 15ml / 1 Tbsp freshly squeezed lemon juice
- 15ml / 1 Tbsp very finely chopped parsley
- 60ml / 4 Tbsp virgin olive oil

* Refer to glossary

Method

Serves 2

1. Peel the artichokes and drop them into a bowl of cold water, that has been acidulated with lemon juice or vinegar.

2. Cook them in salted boiling water until they are tender, drain well and keep on one side.

3. Make the dressing: Grate the lemon zest into a large bowl then add the mustard, honey, lemon juice and chopped parsley. Whisk together using either a balloon whisk or a stick blender. Gradually add the oil, drizzling it in a slow stream while constantly whisking. The dressing should emulsify and thicken. Taste and season as desired with salt and pepper.

4. Cut the bacon into 1cm (½ inch) pieces and fry in a non-stick pan, until crispy.

5. Add the butter and artichokes to the pan and cook to colour them on all sides.

6. Toss the artichokes and bacon in the dressing and serve immediately, piled on a large plate.

Little Bites

ORGANIC FOOD FOR CHILDREN

Mini Traditional
ENGLISH BREAKFAST

A s a child I loved anything in miniature, which is why I have taken a full English breakfast and shrunk it. This microscopic 'fry-up' will tempt any small person. It is the perfect way to set young adventurers up for a secret mission in the woods, a long day of messing around on bikes or an assignment in the snow!

Ingredients
Organic if you can....

YOU WILL NEED:

A small, preferably non-stick, frying pan.

- 4 – 8 pork cocktail sausages or good quality small breakfast sausages
- A little mild olive oil
- 6 rashers of smoked streaky bacon *
- 4 mini plum tomatoes *
- A pinch of caster sugar *
- A pinch of fine sea salt
- 2 quails' eggs or small eggs
- 1 mini brioche loaf or baguette
- A knob / 2 Tbsp of butter
- Parsley to garnish

* Refer to glossary

Method

Serves 2, but these quantities can be modified to suit the size of the appetite and the child.

1. Prick the sausages and cook them in a frying pan with a little oil until they are nicely coloured and crispy on the outside, approximately 10 minutes. Keep warm.

2. Roll up each rasher of bacon and secure with a cocktail stick. Cook in a frying pan until crispy. Keep warm.

3. Prick each tomato a few times, roll in a little olive oil and sprinkle with a pinch of salt and caster sugar. You can cook these in the pan with the bacon, until they are soft. Keep warm.

4. Fry the quails' eggs in a little butter. Slice the brioche and toast it.

5. Serve on a warm plate. Put the egg on a piece of the toasted brioche and arrange the sausages, bacon rolls (remove cocktail sticks) and tomatoes around it. Garnish with a tiny piece of parsley.

Tomato Soup
WITH CHEESY TEDDY BEAR CROUTONS

C hildren love dunking the little teddy croutons into their soup, making patterns with the Greek Yoghurt as they stir it in and also having their own tiny bowl of grated cheese to sprinkle on top. If you have alphabet cutters you can have fun spelling the child's name or writing 'eat me' in tiny cut-outs of buttered toast. A bowl of healthy soup goes down even more readily with a little distraction!

Ingredients
Organic if you can....

- 1 onion
- ½ leek
- 1 carrot
- 30ml / 2 Tbsp mild olive oil
- 800g / 1lb 12oz tin of plum tomatoes *
- 2 sprigs of fresh thyme
- Salt and freshly ground black pepper
- 10ml / 2 tsp brown sugar

FOR THE CROUTONS:
- 6 slices wholemeal bread
- A little butter
- 30g / 1oz grated Cheddar cheese (4 Tbsp)

TO SERVE:
- 60ml / 6 dessert spoons Greek yoghurt (¼ cup)
- 85g / 3oz grated cheddar cheese (¾ cup)
- 6 sprigs of Greek basil, with tiny leaves

* Refer to glossary

Method

Makes 6 children's portions

1. Wash the vegetables, finely chop the onion and leek and grate the carrot.

2. Warm the olive oil in a heavy-based pan, add the vegetables. Cook with the lid on for 5–10 minutes until they are soft, but do not allow them to colour.

3. Add the tomatoes and thyme, and season with salt, pepper and sugar. Bring to a gentle simmer. Cook with the lid on for a further 30 minutes, stirring every so often.

4. Leave to cool a little, remove the sprigs of thyme and then blend half the soup to a smooth creamy consistency using a stick blender or liquidiser. Return the blended soup to the pan and mix well. Some children prefer a smooth soup with 'no bits' in it, in which case you can blend all of it.

5. To make the croutons: Preheat the oven to 180ºC / 350ºF. Butter the bread on both sides. Using a teddy shaped cutter, cut out 3 or 4 croutons for each child.

6. Sprinkle them with the grated cheese, place on a baking tray and bake for 10-12 minutes, until they are crisp and golden.

7. Serve the soup into warm bowls, top each one with a dessert spoon of Greek yoghurt and a sprig of basil. Serve with tiny individual bowls of finely grated cheddar cheese and the teddy croutons.

This is a super quick supper to throw together, especially if you already have some home-made pesto in the refrigerator. From no age at all, my girls have loved stripping the basil leaves from their stems to make pesto. They have grown to love the smell of the basil on their hands and I believe that learning to appreciate all aspects of food – tastes, textures, colours and smells – is the very best way of encouraging children to be adventurous with their food, both preparing and eating it.

You will not need all of the pesto in this recipe for this dish, but it is not practical to make a smaller quantity in a food processor. You can store the remainder in the refrigerator for up to a week.

Orzo With Pesto
AND PARMESAN CRISPS

Ingredients
Organic if you can....

YOU WILL NEED:
A medium baking tray, either non-stick or lined with a silicon mat or baking parchment.

FOR THE PESTO:
- 30g / 1oz pine nuts * (¼ cup)
- 55g / 2oz parmesan, grated (½ cup)
- 1 small clove of garlic
- 55g / 2oz basil leaves (¾ cup packed)
- 75ml / 5 Tbsp virgin olive oil
- Freshly ground black pepper

FOR THE PARMESAN CRISPS:
- 55g / 2oz parmesan cheese, grated (½ cup)

TO SERVE:
- 85g / 3oz orzo (½ cup)
- 60ml / 4 Tbsp crème fraîche

* Refer to glossary

Method

Serves 2

1. To make the pesto: Toast the pine nuts lightly in a frying pan. Transfer them to a food processor or blender and process them, with the parmesan and garlic, to a smooth consistency.

2. Add the basil, olive oil and a few twists of black pepper. Process again to blend all the ingredients together.

3. Store in a glass jar, with a layer of olive oil on the top to prevent discolouration. Keeps in the fridge for up to a week.

4. Preheat the oven to 180ºC / 350ºF.

5. To make the parmesan crisps: Place 6 small heaps of the grated parmesan onto the baking tray or silicon mat. Spread each one out to a circle with a diameter of approximately 8cm (3¼ inches). Try not to leave any holes or gaps in the circles of parmesan, or the crisps are more likely to break when they are cooked.

6. Bake for 10–12 minutes, until all the cheese has melted and they are starting to colour slightly.

7. Leave to cool on the baking sheet for a minute before carefully removing them with a palette knife or spatula and draping them over a rolling pin to shape them as they harden. These are best eaten on the day that they are made, as they quickly lose their crispness and become chewy.

8. To serve, cook the orzo for 10 minutes (or as directed on the packet) and drain through a sieve.

9. Warm the crème fraîche in the same saucepan. Add the drained orzo back into the pan and stir to combine, then stir in 6 tablespoons of pesto.

10. Spoon into warmed bowls and serve immediately.

11. Finish with a parmesan crisp and tiny sprig of basil. Serve extra parmesan crisps on the side.

Little Sausage Man
AND MASH

Children seldom need encouragement to tuck into sausages and mash; even so, I love to surprise them with this little chap. He has brought smiles to many little faces over the years. He is perfect for any nursery menu, but he has also been known to venture out on picnics; as a cold sausage man! He is very easy to make, but you should be on hand to remove the cocktail sticks that hold him together.

Ingredients
Organic if you can....

YOU WILL NEED:

6 cocktail sticks or toothpicks

FOR THE SAUSAGE MEN:

- 10 pork cocktail sausages
  (or good quality small breakfast sausages)
- A little light olive oil
- 2 cherry tomatoes
- 2 button mushrooms or the ends of a
  cucumber (for hats)
- 6 small pieces of broccoli

FOR THE MASH:

- 340g / 12oz floury potatoes
  (1 medium russet potato)
- 75ml / 5 Tbsp milk
- 30g / 2 Tbsp butter
- Salt, pepper and nutmeg

Method

Makes 2 little men, serves 2

1. Heat a little olive oil in a non-stick frying pan. Prick the sausages and cook them for about 10 minutes, until they are nicely browned and crispy. Once cooked, keep warm.

2. While the sausages are cooking, peel and dice the potatoes, and cook them in boiling, salted water until they are soft. Drain thoroughly.

3. Place the milk and butter in the saucepan in which the potatoes were cooked and bring to the boil. Add the potatoes and cook for a minute.

4. Using a fork or potato masher, mash to a very smooth purée and season lightly. I believe that it is important to season children's food carefully and not to serve food that is bland. I use salt sparingly and also a little freshly ground black pepper and finely grated nutmeg, which will lend a very subtle flavour to the potato.

5. Lightly cook the broccoli in salted, boiling water.

6. To assemble the sausage men, you will need one sausage as a body to which you attach two sausages to one end for legs and two sausages at the other end for arms, using the cocktail sticks.

7. For the head, use a tomato, onto which you can secure either a mushroom hat or a cucumber hat. Use another cocktail stick to attach the head and hat to the body.

8. To serve, put a mound of mashed potato onto a warmed plate and either sit or lay the sausage man on it, or you can stand him by propping him up against a high stack of mash. Decorate with 3 pieces of broccoli and serve immediately.

9. I usually accompany him with a tiny bowl of organic tomato ketchup.

Little

SUNDAY ROAST

In England, Sunday lunch at its best is a roast with all the traditional trimmings. Roast chicken was always a favourite on the royal nursery menu. This is a quick, simple and cost effective way to prepare roast chicken when you only need a small quantity and you don't want to roast a whole bird.

Ingredients

Organic if you can....

- 2 boneless chicken breasts
- 4 rashers of streaky bacon *
- 60g / 2oz butter (4 Tbsp)
- 2 small sprigs of fresh thyme
- 2 medium potatoes
- 4 fresh mini corn
- 2 mini courgettes *
- 1 large carrot

* Refer to glossary

Method

Serves 2

1. Preheat the oven to 190ºC / 375ºF.

2. Remove the skin from the chicken. Wrap 2 rashers of bacon neatly around each breast, positioning it so that the ends of the rashers are on the underside; this prevents it from unravelling during cooking.

3. Spread a little butter onto each piece of chicken and place each one on top of a sprig of thyme on a baking tray.

4. Peel and dice the potatoes, then boil them until they are still slightly firm, drain thoroughly. Mix with half of the butter and place in the baking tray with the chicken.

5. Roast everything together for 25–30 minutes.

6. While the chicken and potatoes are roasting, slice the vegetables and cook them lightly in boiling, salted water. Drain, season and mix with a little butter.

7. Pierce the chicken with a skewer to test if it is cooked. If the juices that run out are clear, then it is ready. Leave to stand for 5 minutes before carving it.

8. Slice the chicken thinly and fan it out on a warmed plate alongside the potatoes and vegetables.

9. Serve with a little gravy, if required.

A note from HRH The Princess of Wales requesting roast chicken for lunch, followed by ice cream and fresh fruit salad (FFS)

MEMORANDUM
From ~~The Princess~~ To Carolyn.

Reare and we have roast chicken, peas & roast potatoes, bread sauce for lunch tomorrow - ready for 10 of us!

Many thanks!

D —

Ice-cream +F·F·S? No reare.

Jellies In Oranges,
LEMONS AND LIMES

P arty food! Children are always drawn to these brightly coloured wobbly jellies, just as I was when my mother used to make them for me. They make a glistening display on any party table. You could make your own jelly from fresh fruit juice and gelatine, or you can use 'sugar-free' jellies if you want to offer a slightly healthier option.

Ingredients
Organic if you can....

- 3 oranges
- 3 large, regular shaped lemons
- 3 large, regular shaped limes
- 1 x 135g / 4¾oz packet of blackcurrant jelly *
  (Jell-O)
- 1 x 135g / 4¾oz packet of strawberry jelly *
  (Jell-O)
- 1 x 135g / 4¾oz packet of tangerine or orange
  jelly * (Jell-O)

* Refer to glossary

Method

Makes 36 wedges

1. Wash and dry all the fruit.

2. Cut the fruit in half, be sure to cut the limes and lemons lengthwise.

3. Remove all the flesh from the skins.

4. Rinse and thoroughly dry the insides of the fruit 'shells' (otherwise the jelly will taste extremely bitter).

5. Place fruit shells into a muffin tin; you can wedge each one so that they won't wobble when you fill them with jelly.

6. Dissolve the jelly in 100ml / ⅜ cup of boiling water. Stir in 200ml / ¾ cup of ice-cold water. This makes a slightly firmer jelly than usual, which makes it easier to cut without them collapsing.

7. Fill the oranges with blackcurrant jelly, the limes with tangerine jelly and the lemons with the strawberry jelly. They should be filled right to the very top.

8. Leave to set in the fridge for a couple of hours.

9. Just before serving cut all the jellies in half using a very sharp knife with a long fine blade that has been dipped into hot water. Serve immediately.

I love cooking with children. Meringues have always been a very popular choice with little boys. This is not just because of their enthusiasm to create a menagerie of edible creatures and creepy crawlies, but what small boy (or even young prince) wouldn't be happy armed with a piping bag full of very sticky meringue........?

Animal Meringues

HEDGEHOGS, SNAILS AND MICE

Ingredients
Organic if you can....

YOU WILL NEED:
Two medium baking trays, one piping bag (or if you have three piping bags that is easier as you don't have to change the nozzles)

NOZZLE SIZES:	FOR THE MERINGUE:	FOR THE DECORATION:
• One 1½ cm (½ inch) fluted nozzle for the hedgehogs	• 4 egg whites	• Flaked or slivered almonds for hedgehog prickles
• One 2cm (¾ inch) plain nozzle for the mice	• 225g / 8oz golden caster sugar * (1 cup)	• Liquorice or strawberry strings for mouse tails and snail antennae
• One 1cm (⅜ inch) plain nozzle for the snails	• 2.5 ml / ½ tsp pure vanilla extract *	• Little coloured balls for eyes
	• Natural pink food colouring	* Refer to glossary

Method

Makes 6 - 8 of each animal

1. Preheat the oven to 140ºC / 275ºF.

2. Line the baking trays with non-stick baking parchment.

3. Place the egg whites into a large clean bowl and using either a hand-held electric mixer or stand mixer, whisk until they form 'soft peaks'. They will whisk up best if they are at room temperature.

4. Add the sugar slowly, whisking continuously until the meringue is very thick and glossy, and stands in stiff peaks.

5. Whisk in the vanilla extract.

6. To make the hedgehogs: Spoon ⅓ of the meringue into the piping bag fitted with the fluted nozzle. Pipe a 1cm (½ inch) line and then double back over this to make the body. Then draw away the piping bag to make the pointy nose. To decorate, give the hedgehogs two eyes and plenty of spikes using either slivered almonds or tiny strips of flaked almonds.

7. To make the snails: Spoon another ⅓ of the meringue into the piping bag with the 1cm (½ inch) plain nozzle. Pipe a little blob for the head and then pipe in a spiral motion for the shell. Give each snail eyes and use little pieces of slivered almond or liquorice for the antennae.

8. To make the mice: Mix a drop of pink food colouring into the remaining meringue and then spoon it into the piping bag with the 2cm (¾ inch) plain nozzle. Pipe a 1cm (½ inch) line and then double back over this to make the body. Then draw away the piping bag to make the pointy nose. Give each mouse eyes and a nice long liquorice or strawberry string tail.

9. Bake for approximately 45 minutes, until crisp all through. Check after about 10 minutes and if the meringues are starting to colour, reduce the oven temperature.

10. Cool meringues on baking trays.

11. Store in an airtight container for up to 2 weeks.

Mouse Cupcakes

Ingredients

Organic if you can....

YOU WILL NEED:

12 paper cupcake liners and a 12-hole cupcake tin, or small individual tartlet moulds

FOR THE CUPCAKES:

- 30ml / 2 Tbsp unsweetened cocoa powder
- 115g / 4oz self-raising flour * (1 cup)
- 115g / 4oz golden caster sugar * (½ cup)
- 115g / 4oz soft butter (1 stick)
- 2 free-range eggs (UK medium / USA large) *
- 5ml / 1 tsp pure vanilla extract *

FOR THE CHOCOLATE GLAZE:

- 150g / 5oz milk chocolate (1 cup chocolate drops)
- 85g / 3oz butter (6 Tbsp)

FOR THE DECORATION:

- 12 marshmallows
- Chocolate buttons or flaked almonds (ears)
- Flaked almonds * cut into thin strips (whiskers)
- Miniature marshmallows (eyes and noses)
- Tiny chocolate stars, Smarties or M&M's

* Refer to glossary

Method

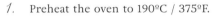

Makes 12 mice

1. Preheat the oven to 190ºC / 375ºF.

2. Place the paper liners into the cupcake tin.

3. Make the cupcakes: Sift the cocoa and flour into a mixing bowl. Add the sugar, butter, eggs and vanilla extract. Beat by hand or with an electric mixer until thoroughly mixed and smooth.

4. Divide the mixture between the paper liners, they should be approximately half full. Scoop out the middle so that when cooked the cupcakes are flat and do not have a peak in the centre.

5. Bake for 12 – 15 minutes, until springy to the touch. Leave to cool.

6. Make the chocolate glaze: Melt the chocolate and stir in the butter to form a very glossy, pourable mixture. As chocolate varies a lot from brand to brand, you may need to add extra chocolate to thicken the glaze.

7. Assemble the mice: If the tops of the cupcakes have risen at all, cut them off so that the top is level. Place a little spot of the chocolate glaze in the centre of each cupcake and then stick a marshmallow onto each one to form the head.

8. Spoon the chocolate glaze over the marshmallow and on the cake so that both are completely covered.

9. Before the chocolate sets, stick the mini marshmallow eyes and nose onto each mouse's head. Also put the ears and whiskers on.

10. You can do further decorating around the top of the cupcake, using the little stars, Smarties or M&M's.

11. Store in an airtight container for up to 3 days.

I love this photo of two very young princes!
Such a special Christmas card.

Wishing you a very Happy Christmas
and New Year
1992

These little mice hold a very special place in my repertoire of children's food as they were the first thing that I made for TRH Prince William and Prince Harry, when they were just 3 and 6 years old respectively. At the time, I was chef to Their Royal Highnesses The Duke and Duchess of Gloucester and the young Princes came to have nursery tea with Lady Davina and Lady Rose. I remember making tiny sandwiches, personalised gingerbread men and these little mice for this very special tea party.

Creamy
VANILLA ICE CREAM

N o ice cream machine is required to make this gorgeously creamy, yet light and fluffy ice cream. All you need is five ingredients and a good whisk or electric mixer. You will not find a commercially made variety that is anywhere near as delicious as this one. This is the ice cream that I grew up on. The recipe came from my wonderful mother, for whom it was never too cold to eat ice cream!

Ingredients
Organic if you can....

- 3 free-range eggs at room temperature (UK medium / USA large) *
- 115g / 4oz golden caster sugar * (½ cup)
- 5ml / 1 tsp pure vanilla extract *
- 200ml / ¾ cup double cream *
- 200ml / ¾ cup crème fraîche

* Refer to glossary

Method

Makes about 8 good servings

1. Place a 1 litre (4 cup) capacity plastic box with a well fitting lid, into the deep freeze to chill.

2. Separate the eggs and keep the whites on one side. Whisk the yolks with the vanilla and ¾ of the sugar in a glass or metal bowl over a pan of hot water, until pale in colour and very thick. Continue whisking off the heat to allow the mixture to cool completely. (If it is still warm when the cream is added, the ice cream will be very dense.)

3. Whisk the cream to soft peaks, whisk in the crème fraîche.

4. Whisk the egg whites until they reach soft peak stage and then add the remaining sugar and keep whisking until you have a very thick and glossy meringue.

5. Carefully fold the cream into the cooled egg yolk mixture.

6. Lastly fold in the meringue, in 3 batches, taking care to mix very lightly.

7. Pour into the pre-chilled box and freeze for several hours before serving.

8. Keeps for up to 4 weeks in the freezer.

Me, an ice cream and bubble loving 3 year old

Tiny
TREACLE TARTS

Ingredients
Organic if you can....

YOU WILL NEED:
20 individual metal tartlet moulds or you can use 2 medium 12 hole muffin pans.

FOR THE PASTRY:
- 120g / 4oz butter (1 stick)
- 30ml / 2 Tbsp golden caster sugar *
- 240g / 8oz plain flour * (2 cups)
- Zest of 1 orange
- 1 free-range egg yolk (UK medium / USA large) *
- 60ml / ¼ cup cold water

FOR THE FILLING:
- 400g / 14oz golden syrup * (1¼ cups)
- 150g / 5½oz fresh white breadcrumbs (3 cups)
- Zest of 1 lemon
- 15ml / 1 Tbsp freshly squeezed lemon juice
- 30ml / 2 Tbsp double cream *

* Refer to glossary

Mummy says its okay !

The note!

Method

Makes 20 small 5cm / 2 inch tarts

1. First make the orange pastry: In a food processor, combine the butter, sugar and flour and process until it resembles breadcrumbs. Grate the orange zest directly into the bowl. Add the egg yolk and a little of the water, whilst pulsing the food processor on and off. Continue adding the water until the dough comes together, but be careful not to over-process or the pastry will be tough when cooked.

2. Remove the pastry from the food processor and on a lightly floured board bring it together into a ball. Wrap and chill for 20 minutes.

3. While it is chilling, warm the golden syrup in a small heavy-based saucepan; do not let it boil. Remove from the heat, add the crumbs and grate the lemon zest in. Leave it to sit so that the crumbs absorb the golden syrup and swell.

4. Remove the pastry from the refrigerator and roll it out on a floured board to a thickness of about 3mm (⅛ inch). Cut out circles to line the tartlet moulds and press the pastry down well into each mould. Chill for a further 15 minutes.

5. Preheat the oven to 180ºC / 350ºF.

6. Add the lemon juice and cream to the golden syrup and breadcrumb mixture.

7. Place a little filling in each tartlet.

8. Decorate the top of each one with small pastry shapes or a lattice of pastry strips. You can also 'personalise' them by putting names on the top using pastry letters.

9. Bake for 15 – 18 minutes. Cool in the moulds for 10 minutes before removing.

10. Serve warm with whipped cream, custard or ice cream or just pop one in your mouth fresh from the oven.

W hen HRH Prince Harry was very young I used to make miniature treacle tarts for him. I kept a
supply of them in the freezer, so that they were available at a moment's notice. Once, when he came
into the kitchen to get one, I asked him to check with HRH The Princess of Wales if he could have
one. He re-appeared moments later with a slip of paper in his hand. It read, 'Mummy says it's ok!' in Princess
Diana's handwriting. I have always treasured this wonderful little note!

Sweet Temptations

DIVINE DESSERTS
&
NOSTALGIC PUDDINGS

Apple & Cinnamon Crumble
WITH BLACKBERRY CREAM

Blackberry and apple crumble is a classic English dessert, and it represents the finest in comfort food. In this recipe I have taken the blackberries out of the crumble and have blended them to a gorgeous velvety purée, which I then fold into whipped cream. The blackberry cream marries perfectly with the warm, comforting apple filling and the crispy, cinnamon-scented crumble topping. (It also makes a very luscious dessert served on its own with shortbread fingers.)

Over the years I have made crumble in many corners of the world. The most exotic location was the Kingdom of Bhutan, which I visited on an official royal tour with HRH The Prince of Wales. His Majesty King Jigme Singye Wangchuck came for dinner and I made a crumble using apples that I had transported from Highgrove and I served it with cream that had also travelled with me, all the way from the Royal Dairy at Windsor.

Ingredients

YOU WILL NEED:

Either four individual portion oven-proof dishes or one 900ml (1½ pint) oven-proof dish

FOR THE APPLE FILLING:

- 900g / 2lbs Bramley apples *
- 40g / 1½oz butter (3 Tbsp)
- 120g / 4oz light muscovado sugar * (½ cup)
- 7.5ml / 1½ tsp cinnamon

FOR THE CRUMBLE TOPPING:

- 120g / 4oz butter (1 stick)
- 60g / 2oz light muscovado sugar * (¼ cup)
- 120g / 4oz plain flour * (1 cup)
- 45g / 1½oz rolled oats (½ cup)
- 30g / 1oz desiccated coconut * (¼ cup)
- 5ml / 1 tsp pure vanilla extract *
- 2.5ml / ½ tsp cinnamon
- 30g / 1oz chopped pecans (¼ heaping cup)

FOR THE BLACKBERRY CREAM:

- 150g / 5½oz blackberries (1 cup)
- 30g / 1oz sugar (2 Tbsp)
- 30ml / 2 Tbsp water
- 5ml / 1 tsp vanilla extract *
- 150ml / ⅔ cup double cream *

* Refer to glossary

Method

Serves 4

1. Preheat the oven to 190ºC / 375ºF.

2. Prepare the apple filling: Peel, core and dice the apples. In a heavy-based saucepan or non-stick frying pan, melt the butter with the sugar and cinnamon. Add the apple and cook it over quite a high heat for about 5 minutes so that it 'caramelises'.

3. Divide the apple between the four oven-proof dishes, or fill one big dish.

4. Make the crumble topping: Place all the ingredients into a food processor and process until the mixture resembles chunky breadcrumbs. (If making it by hand, cream together the butter, sugar and vanilla in a large mixing bowl and then mix in the remaining ingredients).

5. Cover the apple with the crumble mixture.

6. Place the dishes on a baking tray and bake for 20 – 30 minutes depending on the size. The topping should be golden and crunchy.

Continued ➤

Method Continued

7. While the crumble is baking, prepare the blackberry cream: Cook the blackberries with the sugar, water and vanilla in a small saucepan with the lid on, for about 10 minutes, or until the blackberries are soft. Purée them with a hand blender and then rub through a fine sieve to remove the pips.

8. Whip the cream and when the purée is completely cold, swirl it carefully through the cream. Alternatively, you can mix the blackberry purée with Greek yoghurt.

9. Serve the blackberry cream alongside the crumble.

My Tip

When apples are abundant and the hedgerows are glistening with plump blackberries, I recommend picking, preparing and freezing them in small quantities. You can also prepare and freeze the crumble topping and then in the depths of the winter, you can pull some of each out of the freezer, throw them together and in no time you will have a wonderful pudding in the oven!

The blackberry purée also freezes well and it is handy to have a supply of it. I use it in many ways. You can serve it as a warm sauce to go with the crumble or to drizzle over vanilla ice cream. Mixed in with some apple, it is perfect for small children and it makes a nice change from plain apple purée, which they all love. A couple of spoonfuls of purée blended with apple juice, banana, yoghurt and a spoon of wheatbran makes an amazing breakfast smoothie.

"The blackberry cream marries perfectly with the warm, comforting apple filling and the crispy, cinnamon-scented crumble topping."

Apricot
QUEEN OF PUDDINGS

Although this is called 'Queen of Puddings' historically it doesn't have a link to the royal family. Traditionally it is made from white bread and strawberry jam. I use brioche and my home-made apricot jam instead. (You can use commercially made jam if you don't have any that is home-made.) This is the perfect pudding for a cold winter's night – treat yourself like a king and serve it with a jug of thick cream! For children, I love to make little individual puddings baked in small earthenware dishes or ramekins.

Ingredients

YOU WILL NEED:
One 900ml (1½ pint) oven-proof dish, one roasting tin or deep baking tray and one flat baking tray

- 570ml / 2⅓ cups milk
- 115g / 4oz brioche crumbs (1 cup)
- 15g / 1 Tbsp butter + a little extra for the dish
- 30ml / 2 Tbsp light soft brown sugar *
- 5ml / 1 tsp vanilla extract *
- Zest of 1 orange
- 2 free-range eggs (UK medium / USA large) *
- 60ml / 4 Tbsp dried apricot and vanilla jam (see recipe on page 234)
- 55g / 2oz caster sugar * (¼ cup)
- 30g / 1oz flaked almonds * (⅓ cup) OPTIONAL

* Refer to glossary

A tiny note of appreciation

Method

Serves 4 – 6

1. Preheat the oven to 180ºC / 350ºF.

2. Butter the base and sides of the dish.

3. Bring the milk to the boil, remove from the heat and add the brioche crumbs, butter, soft brown sugar and vanilla extract. Finely grate the orange zest into the mixture. Leave to stand for about 30 minutes to allow the brioche crumbs to swell.

4. Separate the eggs, keep the whites on one side. Add the yolks to the mixture and then pour it into the dish.

5. Stand the dish in a deep baking tray or roasting tin, half-filled with water. Bake in the centre of the oven for 35 – 40 minutes, or until it is set, then remove it from the water bath.

6. Spread the jam on top. If it doesn't spread easily, warm the jam gently in the microwave to soften it a little.

7. Whisk the egg whites until stiff and then add in all but 1 tablespoon of the sugar and continue whisking until you have a thick glossy meringue.

8. Pipe or spread the meringue on top of the jam.

9. Sprinkle the remaining sugar and the almonds (if using them) onto the meringue.

10. Place the dish onto a flat baking tray and bake for a further 15 – 20 minutes until the meringue is crisp and golden. Serve immediately.

I love pears... Poached with honey and saffron... Encased in chocolate pastry and smothered in almond frangipane... Served with home-made vanilla ice cream, drizzled with warm chocolate sauce... Filled with Christmas mincemeat, glazed with maple syrup and slowly baked... And especially, caramelised and atop these moist little date and butterscotch puddings...

Caramelised Pear
& DATE PUDDINGS WITH BUTTERSCOTCH SAUCE

Ingredients

YOU WILL NEED:

Four small 150ml (5floz) metal moulds or ramekins, greased and base-lined with baking parchment

FOR THE DATE PUDDINGS:

- 85g / 3oz pitted dates (about 6 dates)
- 100ml / ½ cup water
- 2.5ml / ½ tsp bicarbonate of soda *
- 30g / 2 Tbsp butter + a little extra for the moulds
- 60g / 2oz dark muscovado sugar * (½ cup)
- 1 free-range egg (UK medium / USA large) *
- 5ml / 1 tsp vanilla extract *
- 55g / 2oz plain flour * (½ cup)
- 2.5ml / ½ tsp baking powder
- 30ml / 2 Tbsp ground almonds *

FOR THE CARAMELISED PEARS:

- 4 large ripe, but firm pears
- 60ml / 4 Tbsp caster sugar *
- 30g / 2 Tbsp unsalted butter *

FOR THE BUTTERSCOTCH SAUCE:

(Half the quantity of the recipe on page 233)

* Refer to glossary

A successful pudding!

Method

Makes 4 individual puddings

1. Make the butterscotch sauce and keep on one side.

2. Chop the dates and place them in a small pan with the water, cook until they have softened and broken down. (Dates vary a lot, and some require more cooking than others, in this case you may need to add a little more water.)

3. Remove from the heat, add the bicarbonate of soda; it will bubble up. Leave to subside and to cool.

4. Prepare the pears: Peel and core the pears and slice each one into 6 segments. Caramelise them by melting the butter with the sugar in a non-stick frying pan and cooking the segments carefully until they are tender and golden. Depending on the size of your pan you may need to cook them in two batches.

5. Place 3 pieces of pear in the base of each mould. Keep the remainder on one side for decoration.

6. Make the date puddings: Preheat the oven to 180ºC / 350ºF.

7. Cream the butter and sugar until light and fluffy. Add the cooled date mixture and stir well. Mix in the egg and vanilla. Sift the flour and baking powder into the mixture, add the ground almonds and mix together lightly.

8. Fill each mould almost to the top. Bake for 15 – 20 minutes, remove from the oven and leave the puddings to cool in the moulds for a few minutes.

9. Warm the butterscotch sauce and the caramelised pears.

10. Carefully remove the puddings from the moulds. Place them on pre-warmed dessert plates. Spoon over the warm butterscotch sauce and decorate each plate with pieces of caramelised pear. Serve immediately.

11. You can freeze these puddings once they are cooked. To serve, reheat them in a little of the butterscotch sauce.

Chocolate Orange Mousse
WITH PISTACHIO WAFERS

I believe that a good cookbook needs a great chocolate mousse recipe. This is one of the first things that I made at cookery school and it is a recipe that I always come back to; the mousse is light in texture and not too rich. You can use dark, milk or white chocolate (reduce the quantity of sugar by half with white and milk chocolate). Layers of dark, milk and white chocolate mousse presented in a tall glass make an elegant dessert. Use the best quality chocolate that you can lay your hands on – I love the flavour of Valhrona.

When I first made this mousse, I loved painstakingly painting melted chocolate onto rose leaves, then when the chocolate had set, peeling the leaves off. Making my own chocolate leaves was definitely worth the time and effort. However, when time is of the essence, you can still make things look pretty with simpler garnishes, such as the chocolate scrolls that I have used here.

Ingredients

YOU WILL NEED:
Four mugs or six small cups or one large glass serving bowl

FOR THE PISTACHIO WAFERS:	FOR THE MOUSSE:	FOR THE DECORATION:
Makes thirty 5cm / 2 inch rounds	• 3 leaves gelatine ** OR 7.5ml / 1½ tsp powdered gelatine ***	• 100ml / ½ cup double cream *
• 60g / 2oz butter (4 Tbsp)	• 300ml / 1¼ cups milk	• 12 white chocolate scrolls or chocolate 'Flakes'
• 2 free-range egg whites (UK medium / USA large) *	• 115g / 4oz dark chocolate	• A little extra orange zest
• 60g / 2oz caster sugar * (4 Tbsp)	• 2 free-range eggs, separated (UK medium / USA large) *	• A little cocoa powder for dusting
• 60g / 2oz plain flour * (4 Tbsp)	• 30g / 1oz caster sugar * (4 Tbsp)	* Refer to glossary
• 60g / 2oz ground pistachios (4 Tbsp)	• Zest of 1 orange	** Reduce this to 2 leaves if making the mousse more than 8 hours ahead
• 2.5ml / ½ tsp pure vanilla extract *	• 150ml / ⅔ cup double cream *	*** Reduce to 5ml / 1 tsp if making more than 8 hours ahead.
	• 45ml / 3 Tbsp Cointreau liqueur	

Method

Makes 4 generous or 6 small servings

1. Make the wafers: Preheat the oven to 190ºC / 375ºF.

2. Melt the butter and allow to cool.

3. Whisk the egg whites until stiff and then add the sugar and continue whisking until thick and glossy.

4. Sift the flour onto the meringue and fold in, together with the melted butter, two-thirds of the pistachios and the vanilla extract.

Continued ➤

"I believe that a good cookbook needs a great chocolate mousse recipe. This is one of the first things that I made at cookery school and it is a recipe that I always come back to."

Method Continued

5. Spread the mixture onto silicon baking sheets or baking parchment in thin 5cm (2 inch) rounds (or bigger if you like!) Sprinkle with the remaining pistachios.

6. Bake for 3 – 5 minutes, until they turn a light golden colour. Cool on a wire rack. Alternatively, as soon as they come out of the oven and are still soft, drape them over a rolling pin to create an attractive shape.

7. When completely cold, transfer the wafers to an airtight container and store until required.

8. Make the mousse: Place the gelatine leaves in cold water to soften for at least 5 minutes. (If using powdered gelatine, mix it with 2 tablespoons of cold water and leave to hydrate for several minutes).

9. Cream the egg yolks with the sugar.

10. Heat the milk in a small heavy-based pan with the chocolate. Stir to dissolve the chocolate. Pour the warm chocolate milk onto the egg yolks and whisk. Return the mixture to the pan and heat gently to thicken. Don't let it boil, or it will curdle.

11. When it is thick enough to coat the back of a metal spoon, remove from the heat. Add the orange zest and the Cointreau.

12. If using leaf gelatine, squeeze out the excess water and mix it into the hot mixture. Stir thoroughly. (If using powdered gelatine, add 5 tablespoons of the hot chocolate milk to the hydrated powdered gelatine and mix well and then return this to the pan and stir thoroughly to ensure that there are no lumps).

13. Pour the mixture into a large bowl and place it in a water bath to cool. Once cool, place it in the refrigerator for 10 to 15 minutes until it starts to thicken. (If it begins to set, place the bowl in warm water to loosen the mixture again.)

14. Whip the cream lightly, to form soft peaks, and fold it into the mousse.

15. Whip the egg whites until stiff, then fold them into the mousse in three batches. Mix carefully to achieve a light and fluffy mousse.

16. Pour into serving dishes and chill for at least one hour.

17. Decorate each one with a rosette of whipped cream, two chocolate scrolls, a little very fine orange zest and a dusting of cocoa powder.

18. Serve with pistachio wafers.

Graduation from cookery school!

Eton Mess

I love everything about this dish – the name, the ingredients, the endless possibilities and particularly the many tales surrounding its origins. One of those tales relates how an over-excited Golden Labrador allegedly jumped onto a perfect Strawberry Pavlova that was about to be enjoyed by parents at an Eton College open day picnic. This resulted in the now famous 'Eton Mess' - a jumble of summer fruits, cream and shattered meringues. Many years later, Eton College was attended by TRH Prince William and Prince Harry.

This is my interpretation of Eton Mess, but however you choose to combine and present summer fruits with cream and meringues you will end up with something luscious and indulgent!

Ingredients

YOU WILL NEED:

2 medium baking trays lined with non-stick silicon mats or baking parchment, 1 piping bag with medium fluted star nozzle, 1 piping bag with a small plain nozzle.

FOR THE MERINGUE:

- 3 free-range egg whites (UK medium / USA large) *
- 85g / 3oz white caster sugar * (6 Tbsp)
- 85g / 3oz golden caster sugar * (6 Tbsp) OR you can use ¼ cup in total of granulated sugar
- A few drops of pure vanilla extract *

FOR THE FILLING:

- 225g / 8oz mixed strawberries, blueberries and raspberries (2 cups)
- 225ml / 1 cup double cream *
- 110ml / ½ cup mascarpone
- 30ml / 2 Tbsp caster sugar *
- A handful of mint leaves
- Icing sugar *

FOR THE PURÉE:

- 110ml / ½ cup of raspberry purée (made by blending 115g (4oz) raspberries with 30ml (2 Tbsp) icing sugar and a few drops of lemon juice. After blending, rub through a fine sieve to remove all pips, then add 4 fresh mint leaves and blend again.)

* Refer to glossary

Method

Serves 4

1. Set the oven to 160ºC / 325ºF.

2. Line two baking trays with non-stick baking parchment. Onto the parchment draw 4 circles in each of the following sizes: 2cm, 4cm, 6cm, 8cm and 10cm, (¾, 1½, 2½, 3¼ and 4 inches).

3. Make the meringues: In a clean dry bowl, whisk the egg whites until stiff. Add the sugar and the vanilla extract while continuing to whisk, to yield a firm and glossy meringue. Spoon the meringue into the piping bag with a medium nozzle and pipe it thinly onto the circles on the baking parchment.

4. Bake for 30 – 40 minutes until firm and crisp, but do not allow them to colour. Turn off the oven and leave them in.

5. You can make these up to a week in advance. Store in an airtight container.

6. Assemble the Eton Mess: Wash, dry and prepare all the berries Shred the mint finely, leaving a few leaves whole for the garnish.

7. Whip the cream with the mascarpone and sugar, mix in the mint. Spoon the cream into the piping bag with a small nozzle.

8. Assemble the Eton Mess on the plates that you will be serving it on. Beginning with the largest meringue disc, pipe a little cream onto it and arrange some raspberries neatly on top of the cream. Top with the 8cm disc, pipe cream onto it and neatly arrange some blueberries. Repeat the process 3 more times with the three remaining discs, topping them with strawberry pieces, blueberries and top with a single raspberry, as in the photograph. Repeat the process three more times. Don't assemble the Eton mess more than an hour before you are going to serve it as the meringues soften.

9. Just before serving, drizzle each tower with raspberry purée, garnish with mint leaves and dust with icing sugar.

Iced

GINGER MERINGUE

*J*ust as my ginger cake has a feisty hit of ginger, so too does this frozen delight. I love it for its sheer simplicity; all you need is meringues, whipped cream, a good measure of ginger, some orange zest and a deepfreeze. Served with a salad of minted tropical fruit, it is ideal for a celebratory summer luncheon in the garden. You can also wrap it in ice packs, pop it in a cooler box and impress family and friends by producing it at a picnic.

Ingredients

YOU WILL NEED:

One 600ml / 1 pint china pudding basin and one large baking sheet lined with non-stick baking parchment.

FOR THE MERINGUES:

- 2 free-range egg whites (UK medium / USA large) *
- 90g / 3oz golden caster sugar * (6 Tbsp)
- 30g / 1oz demerara sugar * (2 Tbsp)

FOR THE GINGER CREAM:

- 300ml / 1¼ cup double cream *
- Zest of 1 un-waxed lemon *
- Zest of 1 orange
- 3 pieces stem ginger *
- 30g / 1oz crystallised ginger
- 30ml / 2 Tbsp The King's Ginger liqueur

FOR THE MINTED PINEAPPLE SALAD:

- 1 small, sweet pineapple
- 2 passion fruit
- A handful of mint leaves

* Refer to glossary

Method

Serves 4 – 6

1. Make the meringues:
Preheat the oven to
130ºC / 250ºF. Whisk the egg whites until stiff. Add the sugar slowly while continuing to whisk, to yield a firm and glossy meringue.

2. Spoon the meringue into 10 mounds on the baking tray and sprinkle with the demerara sugar. Bake for 1 hour if they are not crisp after this time, then cook for a little longer. Once cooked, turn off the oven and leave them in while it cools down.

3. Line the pudding basin with cling film* and put it in the freezer to chill.

4. Whip the cream until it stands in soft peaks. Don't over whip it or you will spoil the texture of the frozen dessert.

5. Crush the meringues roughly and mix them into the cream. Finely grate the citrus zest, stem ginger and crystallised ginger into the cream with the ginger liqueur and mix together.

6. Spoon the mixture into the pudding basin and pack down well. Cover and freeze for 3 – 4 hours.

7. Dice the pineapple and combine it with the passion fruit and mint leaves.

8. To serve, turn out the iced meringue onto a plate and accompany it with the fruit salad.

Chilled Lemon Tart

WITH STRAWBERRY SALAD

This lemon tart provides the perfect finalé to a special meal. It has a biscuit-crumb base and a chilled filling that make it a lot quicker to prepare than the traditional baked lemon tart with a pastry crust. For the base you can use your favourite sweet biscuits: McVitie's Digestives, Walkers shortbread fingers or Graham crackers all work well. Serve the tart with a summery, minted strawberry salad and the vibrant red berries next to the fresh, lemon-yellow filling will leap off the plate at you shouting, 'Eat me!'

Ingredients

YOU WILL NEED:

One 15 – 18cm (6 – 7 inch) flan ring or china flan dish

FOR THE BASE:

- 140g / 5oz sweet biscuits * (1½ cups)
- 70g / 2½oz butter (5 Tbsp)

FOR THE FILLING:

- 150ml / ½ cup double cream *
- 1 x 397g / 14oz tin * sweetened condensed milk
- 3 lemons, zest and juice

FOR THE STRAWBERRY SALAD:

- 200g / 7oz strawberries
- 100g / 3½oz raspberries
- 30ml / 2 tablespoons icing sugar *
- A few drops of lemon juice
- A few stems of mint

* Refer to glossary

Method

Makes one 15 – 18 cm (6 – 7 inch) tart, 4 - 6 servings

1. Make the base: Crush the biscuits, melt the butter and mix them together. (The type of biscuits you use will determine how much melted butter will be needed to bind the base.)

2. Press the biscuit mixture into the base of the flan ring or dish, and chill.

3. Make the filling: Whip the cream and fold it into the condensed milk.

4. Grate the lemon zest directly onto the cream mixture and stir it in with the lemon juice.

5. Pile the filling onto the crumb base. Level the top, cover and chill for at least an hour.

6. Make the strawberry salad: Wash, hull and slice the strawberries and place them in a bowl.

7. Crush the raspberries with the icing sugar and lemon juice and rub them through a sieve to make a smooth purée. Drizzle the purée over the strawberries. Shred the mint and sprinkle it onto the fruit.

8. Transfer the tart to a pretty plate, remove the flan ring and serve with the strawberry salad.

Lemon & Lime Posset

WITH SESAME SHARDS, FRESH BLUEBERRIES AND LITTLE VANILLA SHORTBREAD FINGERS

F or a very quick and simple dessert, serve the posset on its own. Presented with all the accompaniments, it becomes a special occasion dessert. The combination of creamy posset, crunchy sesame shards, tangy blueberries and buttery vanilla shortbread fingers is divine!

Ingredients

YOU WILL NEED:

6 ramekins or demi-tasse cups, One baking tray with a silicon sheet or non-stick baking parchment

FOR THE POSSET:

- 500ml / 2 cups double cream *
- 110ml / ½ cup milk
- 140g / 5oz caster sugar * (¾ cup)
- 30ml / 2 Tbsp freshly pressed lemon juice
- 30ml / 2 Tbsp freshly pressed lime juice
- Zest of 1 lime
- Zest of 1 un-waxed lemon *

FOR THE SESAME CARAMEL SHARDS:

- 115g / 4oz caster sugar * (½ cup)
- 60ml / 4 Tbsp water
- 30g / 2 Tbsp sesame seeds

VANILLA SHORTBREAD FINGERS:

- (See recipe for Variations on Chocolate Orange Shortbread Fingers on page 160)
- 200g / 7oz fresh blueberries

* Refer to glossary

Method

Serves 4

1. Make the shortbread fingers.

2. Make the posset: Bring the cream, milk and sugar to the boil and simmer for 3 minutes. Watch it closely as it boils over easily.

3. Remove from the heat, grate the citrus zest directly into the cream and add the citrus juice, stir well.

4. Pour the mixture into the ramekins or cups. Leave to cool before putting in the refrigerator to chill for 2 – 3 hours.

5. Make the sesame caramel shards: Place the sugar and water in a small heavy-based pan on a medium heat.

6. Stir to dissolve the sugar and then allow to simmer until it becomes a rich gold colour. (Keep a close eye on it as it very quickly darkens and burns.)

7. Add the sesame seeds and then pour out in a thin layer onto the baking tray lined with a silicon sheet.

8. Leave for about 15 minutes to harden, before breaking it into small shards. If it is a damp or humid day it should be moved into an air-tight container as soon as it is cold and hard or it will quickly become soft and sticky.

9. Present the posset on a dessert plate, spiked a couple of caramel shards and accompanied by the blueberries and shortbread fingers.

A Trifle Royal

T rifle purists might argue that this is not really a trifle at all. I admit to trifling with the ingredients: replacing sponge cake with Amaretti biscuits, custard with blackberry cream and sherry with Cassis, but regardless of its questionable authenticity, people always come back for more.

Trifle has a very special association for me. On December 16th 1997, my mother accompanied me to Buckingham Palace to the Christmas dance given by Her Majesty the Queen and His Royal Highness The Duke of Edinburgh. During the evening, Her Majesty exchanged a few words with my mother, after which we sat down to pinch ourselves – were we really were sitting in the grandeur of the Throne Room in the heart of Buckingham Palace? When dessert was served, there were amongst other things, individual trifles served in glasses. My mother proclaimed that, in all of her 86 years, a trifle had never tasted so good.

Ingredients

YOU WILL NEED:

Four stem glasses or tumblers

- 1 x 135g / 4¾oz packet of strawberry jelly *
  (Jell-O) made up with 450ml (1¾ cups)
  water and set in a shallow dish
- 120g / 4oz small strawberries (1 cup)
- 120g / 4oz raspberries (1 cup)
- 120g / 4oz blueberries (1 cup)
- 120g / 4oz blackberries (1 cup)
- 60g / 2oz caster sugar * (4 Tbsp)
- 2.5ml / ½ tsp vanilla essence
- 300ml / 1⅓ cup double cream *
- 20 crisp Amaretti biscuits (120g / 3oz)
- 60ml / 4 Tbsp Cassis
- A handful of mint leaves
- 4 small sprigs of mint

* Refer to glossary

EⅡR

*The Master of the Household
has received Her Majesty's command to invite*

Mrs Carolyn Robb

*to a Dance to be given at Buckingham Palace
by The Queen and The Duke of Edinburgh
on Tuesday, 16th December, 1997 at 8.30 p.m.*

Dress: Dinner Jacket
or
Lounge Suit

This card does not admit

Invitation to the Palace!

Method

Serves 4

1. Make up the jelly and leave it to set. You should do this several hours before you start preparing the rest of the trifle.

2. Prepare the strawberries, raspberries and blueberries by washing, drying and hulling where necessary. Reserve a handful of the best ones for decoration.

3. Cook the blackberries in a little water with half the sugar and the vanilla. When soft, purée with a stick blender and rub through a sieve to remove the pips. Keep on one side.

4. Whip the cream with the remaining sugar.

5. Once the jelly has set, dice it into small squares and divide half of it between the 4 glasses.

6. Add a layer of whipped cream, using one third of the cream divided between the 4 glasses.

7. Crush the Amaretti and sprinkle half of the crumbs on to the cream.

8. Divide the remaining jelly between the 4 glasses and top with a layer of blueberries and raspberries, drizzle with the Cassis.

9. Mix the blackberry purée into half of the remaining whipped cream and spoon it onto the fruit, dividing it between the 4 glasses.

10. Sprinkle with the remaining crushed Amaretti and add a layer of sliced strawberries. Chill for at least 30 minutes.

11. When ready to serve the trifle, shred the mint leaves finely and fold them into the remaining whipped cream. Spread the cream onto the top of each trifle and decorate with a few berries and a small sprig of mint.

Cookies & Small Confections

TANTALISING TEATIME TREATS INSPIRED BY MY CHILDHOOD AND MY TRAVELS

Almond Frangipane Bites
WITH BLUEBERRIES

Straight from the oven, these little nuggets are irresistible. They are crunchy on the outside with aromatic, buttery frangipane inside and they have little explosions of juicy blueberry throughout. I challenge anyone to eat just one! You can use fresh or frozen blueberries. If you have fresh ones you should freeze them for at least 30 minutes before mixing them into the frangipane. This prevents the juice from running out when you bake them. For a festive version of this recipe you can substitute the blueberries with some vine fruits soaked in rum or brandy.

Ingredients

YOU WILL NEED:
About 20 small metal or silicon moulds of any shape OR you can use a mini muffin tin.

- A little soft butter for buttering the moulds
- 115g / 4oz soft butter (1 stick)
- 115g / 4oz golden caster sugar * (½ cup)
- 2 free-range eggs (UK medium / USA large) *
- 30g / 1oz plain flour * (¼ cup)
- 115g / 4oz ground almonds * (1 cup)
- 15ml / 1 Tbsp Kirsch, brandy or cherry brandy
- 5ml / 1 tsp pure vanilla extract *
- 100g / 3½oz frozen blueberries (¾ cup)

* Refer to glossary

Method

Makes 15 – 20 depending on size of moulds

1. Preheat the oven to 180ºC / 350ºF.

2. Butter the moulds very thoroughly.

3. Cream together the butter and sugar until light and fluffy.

4. Beat the eggs and add them to the butter and sugar gradually, with 1 tablespoon of flour.

5. Mix in the ground almonds, remaining flour, Kirsch and vanilla extract.

6. Spoon the mixture into the moulds.

7. Press a few frozen blueberries into the mixture in each mould and sprinkle with flaked almonds.

8. Bake for 10–15 minutes, depending on size.

9. Leave to cool for a few minutes before removing from the moulds.

10. Just before serving dust with icing sugar.

11. Store in an airtight container in the fridge for up to 3 days. Gently microwave them or pop them in the oven for a few minutes to warm them through before serving them.

Method Continued

10. Bake both batches of shortbread for 12 – 15 minutes. The orange shortbread fingers should be evenly golden coloured.

11. Remove from the oven, leave to cool on the baking trays for a few minutes before transferring them to a wire cooling rack.

12. Remove the chocolate cream from the refrigerator and beat it until it becomes light and fluffy, but be careful as it can become grainy if over-mixed. Use at once as it will start to thicken quickly.

13. Place the filling in the piping bag with a small fluted nozzle. Pipe a stripe of chocolate along the length of each of the chocolate fingers and then sandwich each one together with an orange finger.

14. Leave to firm up before storing in an airtight container. They keep for up to 4 days, but are at their best on the day they are made.

15. Dust with icing sugar or cocoa powder just before serving.

Variation

For traditional Viennese-style shortbread fingers leave out the orange zest and replace the cocoa powder with the same weight in flour. These are perfect to serve with coffee or to accompany desserts, such as crème brûlée and lemon posset.

"I love to include shortbread in an afternoon tea spread, and if you should happen to be serving tea in Scotland, perhaps in a castle in the Highlands, then it's essential!"

Coconut, Cornflake
AND CHERRY MACAROONS
(GLUTEN FREE & DAIRY FREE)

These simple, rustic macaroons are very quick to whip up. My mother often made them for me as a child when I had friends coming to play, and they all loved them. I remember how much I enjoyed peeling the rice paper off the macaroons and eating it! It's not always easy to find, but some supermarkets do sell small packs of edible rice paper. It is worth taking the time to toast the coconut before adding it to the mixture as it gives the macaroons a lovely buttery-nutty flavour. If you are making these for someone with a gluten intolerance it is important to note that not all cornflakes are gluten free, you do have to buy those that are labelled as GF.

Ingredients

YOU WILL NEED:
2 medium baking trays

- 85g / 3oz desiccated coconut * (⅔ cup)
- 2 free-range egg whites (UK medium / USA large) *
- 180g / 6oz caster sugar * (¾ cup)
- 5ml / 1 tsp pure vanilla extract *
- 85g / 3oz gluten-free cornflakes (3 cups)
- 85g / 3oz glacé cherries * (⅓ cup)
  You could also use maraschino cherries.
- Squares of rice paper, approx 5cm (2 inches) square

* Refer to glossary

Method

Makes about 15

1. Preheat the oven to 170ºC / 325ºF.

2. Lay the squares of rice paper onto the baking trays. If not using rice paper, line the baking trays with either a silicon mat or with non-stick baking parchment.

3. Toast the coconut on a small baking tray in the oven for about 5 minutes, it should be very light golden in colour.

4. Rinse the sticky syrup off the glacé cherries, then dry them and finely slice them.

5. Place the egg whites in a large, clean, dry bowl and whisk until stiff. Gradually add the sugar while continuing to whisk, until you have a very thick glossy meringue.

6. Fold in the vanilla, coconut, cornflakes and cherries.

7. Place spoonfuls onto the rice paper or onto the prepared baking trays.

8. Bake for 15–20 minutes, until the macaroons are firm but not coloured.

9. Cool on a wire rack. Store in an airtight container for up to a week.

10. You can decorate the macaroons with a drizzle of melted dark chocolate or make mini macaroons, half dip them in chocolate and pack them into a small Kilner jar for a lovely gift.

Date Flapjacks

(GLUTEN FREE)

T raditionally flapjacks do have a lot of sugar in them but in this recipe I have replaced some of the sugar with dates. I cook them in butter and golden syrup until they form a sticky 'butterscotch sauce', which then binds all the ingredients together. These flapjacks are great for coeliacs, provided that you use oats that are certified as gluten free.

Ingredients

YOU WILL NEED:

One 20cm (8 inch) square cake tin

- 200g / 7oz pitted dates (1¼ cups)
- 285g / 10oz butter (2½ sticks)
- 140g / 5oz golden syrup * (⅓ cup + 2 Tbsp)
- 30g / 2 Tbsp dark muscovado * sugar
- 200g / 7oz gluten-free rolled oats (2⅓ cups)
- 85g / 3oz gluten-free jumbo oats (1 cup)
- 30g / 1oz unsweetened desiccated coconut * (¼ cup)
- 30g / 4 Tbsp linseed *
- 30g / 4 Tbsp pumpkin seeds
- 5ml / 1 tsp pure vanilla extract *

FOR DECORATION:

- 4 dried apricots
- 15g / 2 Tbsp dried cranberries
- 15g / 2 Tbsp pumpkin seeds

* Refer to glossary

Method

Makes 16 squares or bars or 64 bite-sized morsels

1. Preheat the oven to 170°C / 325°F.

2. Line the base and sides of the cake tin with non-stick baking parchment.

3. Chop the dates and combine them with the butter, golden syrup and sugar in a large heavy-based saucepan.

4. Put on a low heat until the butter melts and then continue to cook gently for several minutes so that the dates break down and you have a thick, gooey mixture.

5. Remove from the heat and stir in the oats, coconut, seeds and vanilla extract. Mix well.

6. Place the mixture into the lined cake tin, do not compact it down too much or the flapjacks will be very dense.

7. Bake for 10 minutes then remove from the oven. Chop the apricots and sprinkle them onto the flapjacks with the cranberries and pumpkin seeds. Cook for a further 5 – 8 minutes. The flapjacks will still be quite soft at this stage but they firm up as they cool.

8. While still just warm, remove the flapjacks from the cake tin using the baking parchment to lift them out. Place them on a chopping board and cut into the required shapes using a sharp serrated pastry knife.

9. When completely cold, store in an airtight container. They keep for up to two weeks.

Jam Drops

T hese take me back to my very early childhood. I remember sitting on the long-legged, wooden kitchen stool happily helping my mother to make the hollows for the jam in the centre of each biscuit, using the handle of a big wooden spoon.

Ingredients

YOU WILL NEED:

2 or 3 medium baking trays

- 120g / 4oz butter (1 stick)
- 140g / 5oz caster sugar * (¾ cup)
- 5ml / 1 tsp pure vanilla extract *
- 2 free-range eggs (UK medium / USA large) *
- 270g / 9½oz self-raising flour * (2¼ cups)
- Passion fruit and strawberry conserve (see recipe on page 250) and dried apricot and vanilla jam (see recipe on page 234) Or any jam of your choice
- A handful of flaked almonds * & finely chopped pistachios
- A little extra caster sugar * for sprinkling on the finished jam drops

* Refer to glossary

Variations

1. For 'Lemon drops' replace the vanilla with the finely grated zest of 1 lemon and fill with home-made lemon curd (see recipe on page 242).

2. For 'Chocolate drops' replace 15g / ½oz of the flour with 15g / ½oz cocoa powder and fill the centres with chocolate hazelnut spread.

Method

Makes approx 12 giant drops, 30 medium drops or 50 mini drops

1. Preheat the oven to 180ºC / 350ºF.

2. Line the baking trays with a silicon mat or non-stick baking parchment.

3. Cream together the butter, sugar and vanilla extract.

4. Mix in the eggs, and 2 tablespoons of the flour.

5. Sift in the remainder of the flour and mix. If the dough is still sticky, add a little more flour. Working lightly, bring the dough together into a ball.

6. Roll the dough into balls between the palms of your hands. For the mini jam drops use a ball of dough the size of a cherry, for medium ones, the size of a walnut and for giant ones the size of an egg.

7. Place onto baking trays, leaving space between them, as they spread during baking.

8. Make an indentation in the centre of each jam drop using the handle of a wooden spoon (dip the end of the handle into flour to prevent the dough from sticking to it). Spoon jam into the hollows.

9. Decorate as desired. Either use individual flaked almonds to form 'petals' around the jam or sprinkle each jam drop with pistachios or simply with some caster sugar.

10. Bake for 8 – 10 minutes, 12 – 15 minutes and 18 – 20 minutes for the small, medium and large sizes, respectively.

11. Leave to cool on the baking trays for a few minutes before transferring to a wire cooling rack.

12. Store in an airtight container for up to a week.

Pistachio Filo Crackers
WITH ORANGE SYRUP

When I lived in Dubai, I passed a wonderful Lebanese bakery on my way to and from work each day. These simple little 'Christmas crackers' are inspired by my many visits to the Al Reef Bakery (for my favourite hot cheese and Zatar bread or just for a square of baklava). Classic baklava is made with eight layers of special paper-thin pastry dough, clarified butter and nuts. Traditionally, in the Middle East, it is associated with celebrations such as weddings, Bar Mitzvahs and Ramadan. I never waited for a celebration as an excuse to eat it! In this very simplified recipe, I mix pistachios with a little honey to bind them together and I add orange zest for its bright colour and tangy flavour. I love to serve these at Christmas time as an alternative to traditional Mince pies.

Ingredients

YOU WILL NEED:

A medium non-stick baking tray or a standard baking tray with a silicon mat.

FOR THE FILLING:

- 115g / 4oz pistachios (1 cup)
- Zest of 1 orange
- 60ml / 4 Tbsp honey

FOR THE PASTRY:

- 3 large sheets of filo pastry measuring 25 x 30cm (10 inches x 12 inches)
- 85g / 3oz butter, melted (6 Tbsp)

FOR THE SYRUP:

- 115g / 4oz caster sugar * (½ cup)
- 75ml / 5 Tbsp water
- Zest of 1 orange
- A few drops of orange flower water
- 15ml / 1 Tbsp of finely chopped pistachios for decoration

* Refer to glossary

Method

Makes 8 small crackers

1. Preheat the oven to 180ºC / 350ºF.

2. Make the nut filling: Chop the pistachios, finely grate the orange zest and mix both with the honey.

3. To assemble the crackers: Lay one sheet of the filo pastry out flat and paint it all over the melted butter. Lay a second sheet on top and paint it as before. And repeat with a third sheet. Cut the pastry into 4 lengthways to make 4 rectangles. Cut these into half to give you 8 squares.

4. Divide the filling into 8 equal amounts and place onto each pastry square in a diagonal strip, but not right to the corners of the pastry.

5. Roll each pastry from corner to corner and squeeze the pastry together at the edge of the filling to create a cracker shape. Paint with a little more melted butter.

6. Bake for 15 – 18 minutes on the middle shelf of the oven.

7. While the crackers are baking, make the syrup: Combine the sugar and water in a small, heavy-based pan. Stir to dissolve the sugar, then boil it for a couple of minutes until it becomes thick and syrupy. Remove from the heat and add the orange zest and orange flower water.

8. Glaze the crackers as soon as they come out of the oven by painting the sugar syrup on using a pastry bush. Chop the pistachios and sprinkle them onto the crackers and add a little extra orange zest if desired.

9. These are most crisp served on the day that they are made.

Triple-Choc
CHOC-CHIP-COOKIES

I lived in California for two years and I grew to love the lifestyle there; the ever-present sunshine, morning runs along the beach with my fellow tri-athletes, copious amounts of incredibly fresh produce from inspiring farmers markets. What more could you want?... A great choc-chip cookie was high on my list and I knew I was in the right place to find one. I tasted a great many in my search for the perfect cookie; it was not an arduous task! This recipe comes very close to my 'top cookie' in California. I recommend using a really good quality chocolate when making these and they are definitely at their best fresh from the oven!

Ingredients

YOU WILL NEED:

3 medium baking trays lined with silicon mats or non-stick baking parchment

- 125g / 4½oz butter (1 stick + 1 Tbsp)
- 225g / 8oz dark soft brown sugar * (1 cup)
- 1 free-range egg (UK medium / USA large) *
- 2.5ml / ½ tsp pure vanilla extract *
- 185g / 6½oz plain flour * (1½ cups)
- 5ml / 1 tsp bicarbonate of soda *
- 30g / 1oz unsweetened, good quality cocoa powder (⅓ cup)
- 70g / 2½oz good quality white chocolate (½ cup chocolate drops)
- 70g / 2½oz good quality dark chocolate (½ cup chocolate drops)
- 1 x 70g / 2½oz Mars bar, roughly chopped and then frozen OR 70g / 2½oz good quality milk chocolate drops OR fudge pieces
- 85g / 3oz white chocolate, melted (¾ cup chocolate drops) - optional

* Refer to glossary

Method

Makes 36

1. Preheat the oven to 180ºC / 350ºF.
2. Cream together the butter, sugar, egg and vanilla extract until light and fluffy.
3. Sift the dry ingredients and mix into the dough. Add the chocolate and frozen Mars bar pieces.
4. Roll teaspoonfuls of the dough into balls and place them on the prepared baking trays, leaving at least 5cm (2 inches) between each cookie to allow for them to spread during baking.
5. Bake for 10 minutes, remove from the oven and leave to stand for a further 2 minutes on the baking trays, before transferring to a wire cooling rack. They will still be very soft when you remove them from the oven, but don't be tempted to cook them for longer as they will become very hard when they cool.
6. When completely cool, you can drizzle the melted white chocolate over them but this is optional, they are just as good without it.

Serving Suggestion

For a special dessert, make giant-sized cookies and serve them straight from the oven – warm, a little chewy and oozing with molten chocolate. Top with a scoop of creamy vanilla ice cream (see recipe on page 123) and drizzle with some Bailey's Irish Cream liqueur.....indulgent but blissful!

Method Continued

10. Spread the dark chocolate all over the cake.

11. Decorate with the Maltesers before the chocolate sets, so that they stick to the cake. Position chocolate sticks as desired and drizzle with the white chocolate.

12. Store in an airtight container in the refrigerator.

13. Keeps for up to 2 weeks, although it seldom lasts that long, once people know that it is there!

Variations

- You can replace the pistachios with pecans, toasted almonds or macadamia nuts.

- You can replace the figs with raisins, sultanas or dried cherries.

- For a festive holiday treat, use glacé cherries and dried apricots that have been soaked in cherry brandy.

- For a children's party cake, decorate with Smarties or M&M's.

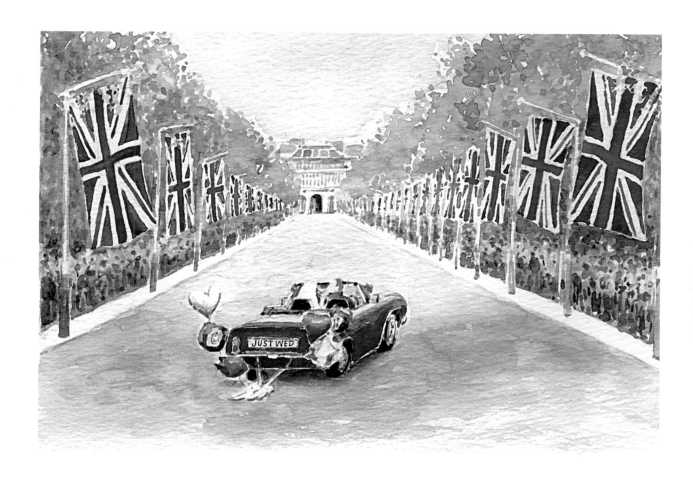

"It was a firm favourite in the royal nursery; so much so that, many years later, Prince William chose to have chocolate biscuit cake at his wedding for the Groom's cake."

Deliciously
MOIST AND RICH GINGER CAKE

Ingredients

YOU WILL NEED:
One deep, round 18cm (7inch) cake tin

FOR THE CAKE:
- 85g / 3oz stem ginger in syrup *
  (this is 3 – 4 pieces)
- 55g / 2oz crystallised ginger (⅔ cup)
- 125g / 4½oz butter (1 stick + 1 Tbsp)
- 200g / 7oz golden syrup * (½ cup)
- 45ml / 3 Tbsp ginger syrup, from the jar of stem ginger
- 125g / 4½oz light muscovado sugar * (⅔ cup)
- 2 free-range eggs (UK medium / USA large) *
- 225ml / 1 cup milk
- 225g / 9oz plain flour * (2 cups)
- 5ml / 1 tsp bicarbonate of soda *
- 10ml / 2 tsp baking powder
- 10ml / 2 tsp ground ginger
- 5ml / 1 tsp ground mixed spice *
- A pinch of paprika
- A pinch of sea salt

FOR GLAZING THE CAKE:
- 50ml / 3 Tbsp golden syrup *
- 2 pieces of stem ginger * cut into paper thin slices

* Refer to glossary

Method

Serves 8 – 10

1. Preheat the oven to 160ºC / 325ºF.

2. Line the base and sides of the cake tin. I use a loose-bottomed, heavy gauge tin.

3. Place the stem ginger and crystallised ginger into a food processor and process to a 'paste'. Alternatively, grate all the ginger finely.

4. Place the butter, golden syrup, ginger syrup, sugar and ginger paste in a heavy-based saucepan. Warm gently, to melt the butter. Stir continuously and do not let it boil. Leave to cool a little.

5. Beat the eggs and milk together and then add them to the warm mixture.

6. Sift together the flour, bicarbonate of soda, baking powder, spices and salt. Mix into the liquid and stir well to ensure that there are absolutely no lumps. Pour the mixture into the prepared tin.

8. Bake for 35 – 45 minutes. The top will become a lovely dark, rich colour. Insert a skewer into the centre of the cake, it will come out completely clean when the cake is cooked.

10. As soon as the cake comes out of the oven, glaze it with the golden syrup and place the fine slivers of stem ginger all over the top of the cake.

11. Leave to cool before removing from the tin.

12. When completely cold, store it in an airtight container and leave to mature for several days before eating.

13. Keeps for up to two weeks.

I use stem ginger, crystallised ginger, ground ginger and a pinch of paprika in this cake, which together give it wonderful kick. There must surely be some health benefits too, in eating this much ginger. It is worth resisting the temptation to delve into this cake fresh out of the oven – if you leave it in an airtight container for several days, the flavours will develop and it will become irresistibly moist and sticky. Don't store it in the refrigerator as it will dry out.

Frosted Orange
MARMALADE CAKE

A s a young child I spent many a happy hour helping my mother in the kitchen. Making marmalade cake together for my father is one of my most treasured memories. It was one of his childhood favourites, made for him by his grandmother. She always made it in a ring mould and to this day, I still only ever make it in this shape, it wouldn't seem right any other way. When Mum and I made this special cake together, we always used Mum's own home-made marmalade, made from our own home-grown citrus that Dad so carefully tended. This is such a special cake on so many levels, with reminiscences that bring a smile to my face, of the most wonderful parents anyone could wish for.

Ingredients

YOU WILL NEED:
A 22cm / 8½ inch ring mould cake tin

FOR THE CAKE:
- A little butter to grease the ring mould
- 225g / 8oz butter (2 sticks)
- 225g / 8oz golden caster sugar * (1⅛ cups)
- 4 free-range eggs (UK medium / USA large) *
- 170g / 8 Tbsp Seville orange marmalade
- Zest of 2 oranges
- 225g / 8oz / plain flour * (1¾ cup)
- 10ml / 2 tsp baking powder

FOR THE ORANGE FROSTING:
- 170g / 6oz icing sugar * (1⅓ cups)
- Zest of 2 oranges
- 45ml / 3 Tbsp freshly pressed orange juice

* Refer to glossary

Method

Serves 10

1. Preheat the oven to 160ºC / 325ºF.

2. Using a knob of soft butter, very thoroughly grease the ring mould, making sure that the centre section and the outside is all covered. Sprinkle a little flour into the mould and toss it around, then tip out any excess.

3. Cream together the butter and sugar until pale in colour and light in texture.

4. Beat the eggs and add them gradually to the butter and sugar with 2 tablespoons of flour, mixing well between each addition.

5. Add the marmalade and grate the orange zest directly into the bowl. Mix well.

6. Sift the remaining flour and baking powder into the mixture and fold it in carefully, with a light hand for a light textured cake! Spoon the mixture into the ring mould.

7. Bake for 35 minutes. To test if it is ready, insert a skewer into the centre of the cake, it will come out clean if the cake is done. At the end of the cooking time, turn off the oven and leave the cake in for a further 10 minutes.

8. Whilst the cake is baking, make the frosting: Sift the icing sugar into a bowl and grate the orange zest into it. Mix the orange juice in gradually, as you may not need all of it. The frosting should be just the right consistency to trickle down the sides of the cake without all running off.

9. Remove the cake carefully from the tin and cool it on a wire rack.

10. Once cold, drizzle the orange frosting over the cake, leave for a short time to harden and decorate with a few fresh flowers in the centre.

11. Stored in an airtight container, it will keep for up to 5 days.

Lime, Raspberry
AND WHITE CHOCOLATE DRIZZLE CAKE

Cut this cake into hearty chunks and take it on a summer's picnic or slice it in delicate fingers and nestle it amongst other dainty morsels on a fine china cake stand for afternoon tea. You can even serve it as a scrumptious dessert – straight from the oven, with clotted cream or crème fraîche. Aromatic limes with tangy raspberries and sweet velvety white chocolate... sheer bliss! I love making this cake in the summer with freshly picked raspberries, but you can make an equally delectable autumnal version by replacing the raspberries with blackberries.

Ingredients

YOU WILL NEED:
One 22cm (9 inch) square cake tin

FOR THE CAKE:
- 200g / 7oz raspberries (1½ cups)
- 225g / 8oz butter (2 sticks)
- 225g / 8oz golden caster sugar * (1 cup)
- 4 free-range eggs (UK medium / USA large) *
- 30g / 1oz ground almonds * (¼ cup)
- 2 limes, zest and juice
- 100g / 3½oz good quality white chocolate, broken into pieces (½ cup)
- 250g / 9oz plain flour * (2 cups)
- 10ml / 2 tsp baking powder

FOR THE LIME SYRUP:
- 85g / 3oz granulated sugar (6 Tbsp)
- Juice of 2 limes
- 45ml / 3 Tbsp boiling water
- 2.5ml / ½ tsp vanilla extract *
- Zest of 1 lime

* Refer to glossary

Method

Makes 12 hearty portions (and many more delicate ones)

1. Before you start, spread the raspberries on a baking sheet and freeze them for about 30 minutes. (If you mix them into the cake batter without freezing them first, they break up and the cake turns bright pink!)

2. Preheat the oven to 160°C / 320°F.

3. Line the base and sides of the cake tin with baking parchment.

4. Cream the butter and sugar together until pale and fluffy. Beat the eggs lightly and add them to the creamed mixture in several batches, mixing well between each addition.

5. Add the ground almonds. Grate the lime zest directly into the mixture and then add the juice and fold in the white chocolate chunks.

6. Sift the flour and baking powder into the bowl and mix. Lastly, add the raspberries, taking care not to break them up.

7. Spoon the mixture into the cake tin. Bake for 35 – 40 minutes, until the cake is firm to the touch and golden in colour. You can also test it with a skewer to be sure it is cooked through.

8. While the cake is baking, make the lime syrup: Combine all the ingredients except the zest in a small heavy-based pan, stir well to dissolve the sugar and then boil for 3 minutes, until it becomes 'syrupy'.

9. As soon as the cake comes out of the oven, prick the surface with a fine skewer. Sprinkle the lime zest onto the cake and spoon the syrup over it.

10. Leave the cake to cool completely and absorb all the syrup before removing it from the tin.

11. This cake is perfect as is, but you can decorate it with a drizzle of melted white chocolate or with fresh raspberries and a dusting of icing sugar.

Cinnamon-Sugar
CAKE

I clearly remember my first play-date at my friend Kim's house. I was five years old. It sticks in my mind, not because of the mischief we got up to, but because of the delicious cake that her mother had baked for tea. I urged my mother to ask for the recipe. Re-named 'Kim-Cake' in our house, it soon became a family favourite. It is at its best, fresh from the oven and still slightly warm, so that the only way to cut it is in chunky, indulgent slices! Try baking it in mini loaf tins to make very appealing little individual loaves.

Ingredients

YOU WILL NEED:

A 900g / 2lb loaf tin, approximately 23 x 13cm, 7cm deep (9 x 5 inches, 2¾ inches deep) or 10 mini loaf tins or disposable loaf moulds (as in the photograph).

FOR THE CAKE:

- 3 free-range eggs, separated (UK medium / USA large) *
- 155g / 5½oz caster sugar * (¾ cup)
- 110ml / ½ cup sunflower oil
- 110ml / ½ cup water
- 140g / 5oz plain flour * (1 cup)
- 15ml / 1 Tbsp cornflour *
- 15ml / 1 Tbsp baking powder
- 10ml / 2 tsp ground cinnamon
- A pinch of salt

FOR THE CINNAMON-SUGAR TOPPING:

- 55g / 2oz butter (4 Tbsp)
- 85g / 3oz golden caster sugar * (½ cup)
- 15ml / 1 Tbsp ground cinnamon

* Refer to glossary

Kim   *Me*

Method

Serves 8 – 10

1. Set the oven to 180ºC / 350ºF.

2. Line the base and sides of the loaf tin with non-stick baking parchment. (The mini disposable loaf moulds don't need lining.)

3. Whisk together the yolks and sugar until light in colour and thick and creamy.

4. Add the oil and water and mix.

5. Sift all the dry ingredients together into the egg mixture and stir well.

6. Whisk the egg whites in a clean, dry bowl with a clean whisk, until they are stiff. Carefully fold them into the mixture in three batches.

7. Pour the mixture into the loaf tin(s) and bang them a couple of times on the kitchen table before you put them in the oven, to remove any large air bubbles.

8. Bake the large loaf for 45 minutes or the mini loaves for 12 – 15 minutes.

9. While the cake is cooking, prepare the topping: Melt the butter and mix in the sugar and cinnamon.

10. Leave the cakes to settle for a few minutes after they come out of the oven and then spread on the topping.

11. When cool, remove from the tin and place on a wire rack, but be careful – it is a light and fragile cake and breaks very easily when it is just out of the oven.

12. Store in an airtight container, best eaten within 3 days.

Our school photo!

Mile-High
MINI VICTORIA SANDWICH CAKES

This cake is about as regal as a cake can be. It was originally made for Queen Victoria. During her incredible 66-year reign, the concept of afternoon tea was created. It evolved and became a daily ritual and a very social event, with ladies dressing in their finery to gather for a cup of tea and an array of tiny sandwiches, biscuits and cakes.

The basic Victoria Sandwich recipe is wonderfully simple and foolproof. I urge you to use really good quality butter, eggs and vanilla. Here is my interpretation, which, I think, might have been a little over-indulgent for Victorian times....

Ingredients

YOU WILL NEED:

1 x 12 hole medium size muffin pan or 12 individual 5cm (2inch) tartlet moulds at least 3cm (1¼ inches) deep.
1 piping bag with a small fluted nozzle.

FOR THE CAKE:

• 115g / 4oz soft butter (1 stick)
• 115g / 4oz golden caster sugar * (½ cup)
• 2 free-range eggs (UK medium / USA large) *
• 115g / 4oz plain flour * (1 cup)
• 7.5ml / 1½ tsp baking powder
• 5ml / 1 tsp pure vanilla extract *
• 15ml / 1 Tbsp boiling water

FOR THE FILLING & DECORATION:

• 225ml / 1 cup double cream *
• 2.5ml / ½ tsp pure vanilla extract *
• 30ml / 2 Tbsp caster sugar *
• 10 large strawberries
• 6 sprigs of fresh mint
• A little extra caster sugar for sprinkling on top

* Refer to glossary

Method

Makes 6 'mile-high' mini Victoria sandwiches

1. Preheat the oven to 180ºC/350ºF.

2. Line the base of each mould with a circle of non-stick baking parchment and butter the sides.

3. Cream together the butter and sugar until light in colour and creamy in texture.

4. Lightly beat the eggs and add gradually to the mixture with 2 tablespoons of the flour.

5. Add the vanilla extract. Sift the remaining flour and baking powder into the mixture and fold it in carefully. Lastly stir in the boiling water.

6. Divide the mixture between the 12 moulds.

7. Bake for 10 – 12 minutes, until the cakes feel springy to the touch.

8. Cool on a wire rack and remove from the tins.

9. Make the filling: Whip the cream with the vanilla and sugar and place ⅓ of it in a piping bag fitted with a small fluted nozzle.

10. Wash, dry and hull the strawberries, then dice them. Wash and dry the mint leaves and chop them finely.

11. Mix half of the diced strawberries and half of the chopped mint into the remaining cream.

12. To assemble: Slice the cakes in half horizontally. Set aside 6 of the 'tops'. Spread the strawberry cream on the remaining cake slices. Stack 3 slices on top of each other and finish with one of the reserved 'top' slices to make a 4-layer mini cake tower. Repeat with the other cake slices.

13. Pipe a rosette of cream on the top of each mini cake tower and top with a little of the diced strawberry and some mint. Sprinkle with caster sugar.

14. These are best eaten on the day they are made, but can be stored overnight in an airtight container in the refrigerator.

Don't be put off by the length of this recipe, it is not difficult to make this cake. I use a hand-held electric mixer for the cake and butter cream, but as long as you use soft butter you can easily make them by hand, and sometimes the cake seems lighter when made this way. The quick-mix coffee and walnut sponge has coffee syrup spooned over it as it emerges from the oven and it is then filled with velvety espresso butter cream, or you can use a chocolate hazelnut spread like Nutella. Finally, it is covered in a dark chocolate glaze and finished in style with a twirl of angled chocolate triangles on the top.

Mocha Gâteau

Ingredients

YOU WILL NEED: Two round 18cm (7 inch) cake tins

FOR THE CAKE:
- 55g / 2oz walnuts (½ cup)
- 170g / 6oz golden caster sugar * (¾ cup)
- 170g / 6oz self raising flour * (1⅓ cup)
- 8ml / 1½ tsp baking powder
- 170g / 6oz soft butter (1½ sticks)
- 3 free-range eggs (UK medium / USA large) *
- 30ml / 2 Tbsp instant espresso powder, dissolved in 30ml / 2 Tbsp boiling water
- 5ml / 1 tsp pure vanilla extract *

FOR THE COFFEE SYRUP:
- 30ml / 2 Tbsp instant espresso powder
- 60g / 2oz light muscovado sugar * (¼ cup)
- 90ml / 6 Tbsp boiling water
- 5ml / 1 tsp pure vanilla extract *

FOR THE BUTTER CREAM:
- 170g / 6oz icing sugar * (1½ cups)
- 90g / 3oz soft butter (6 Tbsp)
- 5ml / 1 tsp pure vanilla extract *
- 15ml / 1 Tbsp instant espresso powder
- A splash of milk - if required

FOR THE CHOCOLATE TRIANGLES:
- 85g / 3oz dark chocolate (½ cup)
- 85g / 3oz cup white chocolate (½ cup)
- 13 Maltesers or small chocolate truffles to decorate

FOR THE CHOCOLATE GLAZE:
- 150g / 5oz good quality dark chocolate
- 100g / 3½oz soft butter (7 Tbsp)

* Refer to glossary

Method

Serves 12

1. Preheat the oven to 180ºC / 350ºF.

2. Line the cake tins with baking parchment.

3. Toast the walnuts in the oven for 5 minutes, then grind them in a food processor or finely chop them. Sift the dry ingredients into a mixing bowl and add the walnuts, butter, eggs, espresso, and vanilla extract then whisk for 2 – 3 minutes until the mixture is thick and homogenous. Divide it between the two tins, spread it evenly with a slight hollow in the centre, and bake in the centre of the oven for 20 – 25 minutes.

4. Prepare the coffee syrup: Place the espresso powder and sugar into a heatproof jug, add the boiling water and vanilla and stir to dissolve the sugar.

5. Prepare the butter cream: Sift the icing sugar into a bowl and add the butter, vanilla and espresso powder. Beat until it is light and fluffy in texture. Add a few drops of milk if it is too thick to spread.

6. Make the chocolate triangles: Draw two 18cm (7 inch) circles onto a piece of baking parchment. Melt the dark and white chocolate separately and spread onto the two circles, as evenly as possible. Leave to harden, in a cool place, but do not refrigerate as it will lose its shine. Using a thin bladed knife or pizza wheel dipped into boiling water, cut each circle into 8 wedges.

7. Prepare the chocolate glaze: Melt the chocolate, then gradually stir in the softened butter. (Chocolate varies a lot from brand to brand, if the glaze is too thin to coat the cake then add more chocolate to thicken it.)

8. When the cakes are cooked, prick them all over with a fine skewer and spoon over the warm espresso syrup. Leave them in their tins to cool.

9. To Assemble: Cut each cake in half horizontally. Using ¾ of the butter cream sandwich the 4 layers together.

10. Cover the top and sides of the cake with the chocolate glaze, by carefully pouring it onto the cake and letting it drizzle down the sides and smooth it with a palette knife. Leave to set at room temperature.

11. Once set, use the remaining butter cream to pipe 12 rosettes around the top of the cake. Place a Malteser on each one and angle the triangles carefully, as in the photograph, alternating between dark and white and leaning them on the Maltesers. Finish with a rosette of butter cream in the centre of the cake.

12. This cake is best eaten fresh. Don't store it in the refrigerator as the glaze will become hard and dull.

Orange Spice Cake
DAIRY FREE

T his cake is very quick and simple to make. It is dairy-free and also gluten free (as long as you use gluten-free bread for the breadcrumbs). For a tempting dessert, serve it with Greek yoghurt and fresh berries or whipped cream with lemon curd folded into it.

Ingredients

YOU WILL NEED:

1 x 20cm (8inch) flan ring, plain or scalloped or a non-stick cake tin

FOR THE CAKE:

- 50g / 2oz breadcrumbs, made from day-old white bread (1 cup)
- 200g / 7oz golden caster sugar * (1 cup)
- 100g / 3½oz ground almonds * (¾ cup)
- 7.5ml / 1½ tsp baking powder
- Zest of 2 oranges
- Zest of 2 limes
- Zest of 1 lemon
- 4 free-range eggs (UK medium / USA large) *
- 200ml / ¾ cup light, mild olive oil

FOR THE SYRUP:

- Juice of 1 orange
- Juice of 1 lime
- Juice of ½ a lemon
- 85g / 3oz golden caster sugar * (6 Tbsp)
- 2 small cinnamon sticks
- 4 cloves
- 4 star anise
- 4 cardamom pods, crushed

* Refer to glossary

Method

Serves 8

1. Line the base of the cake tin with non-stick baking parchment and oil the sides. If using a flan ring, stand it on a silicon baking sheet or baking parchment and oil the sides well.

2. In a large mixing bowl, combine all the ingredients except the eggs and oil.

3. Whisk the eggs and oil together and add them to the dry ingredients, to form a thick batter.

4. Pour the batter into the prepared cake tin and place it on the middle shelf in a cold oven.

5. Then turn the oven on to 190ºC / 375ºF and bake for 20 minutes.

6. After that time, cover the cake with a piece of damp crumpled greaseproof paper or baking parchment to prevent it from getting too brown. Bake for a further 30 minutes.

7. While it is baking make the syrup: Combine all the ingredients in a small heavy-based pan. Stir to dissolve the sugar, then bring to the boil. Reduce the heat and simmer for 2 - 3 minutes. Leave to stand for 15 minutes before removing the spices. Keep them on one side for decorating the cake.

8. When the cake is cooked, let it cool for a few minutes in the tin before turning it out onto a deep serving plate.

9. Pierce all over with a fine skewer or fork and then pour over the syrup, which should be warm. Leave for at least an hour for the cake to absorb the syrup.

10. Decorate with the whole spices before serving.

11. This cake will keep for up to 4 days in an airtight container in the refrigerator.

Rose Petal Cake

This rose petal cake holds a special place in my heart as I made it for my mother's 90th birthday and decorated it with her favourite pink roses from the garden. I love the challenge of making a special birthday cake, particularly if it is for a child and it needs to be a 'Womble', a zebra, a helicopter... or something equally impossible and precarious. I was once commissioned to make a rocket cake for the 3rd birthday of one of HM The Queen's great nephews. I threw caution to the wind and created an impressive red 3-foot tall construction out of sponge cake and butter cream, which I then had to transport 50 miles to London. My wonderful niece Katy nursed it for the entire journey, our hearts were in our mouths each time we went around a corner and it listed dangerously to one side. We all arrived intact and the rocket in perfect condition, ready for blast-off.

Two young princes always managed to come up with ideas for their birthday cakes that pushed the art of constructing something out of cake to the limit!

Ingredients

YOU WILL NEED:

Two round 18cm (7 inch) cake tins

FOR THE FROSTED ROSE PETALS:

- A handful of pink or white rose petals
- 1 free-range egg white lightly beaten (UK medium / USA large) *
- 55g / 2oz caster sugar * (¼ cup)

FOR THE CAKE:

- 225g / 8oz butter (2 sticks)
- 225g / 8oz golden caster sugar * (1 cup)
- 5 free-range eggs, separated (UK medium / USA large) *
- 125g / 4½oz plain flour * (1 cup)
- 7ml / 1¼ tsp baking powder
- 125g / 4½oz ground almonds * (1 cup)
- 5ml / 1 tsp natural almond essence *
- A few drops of natural pink colouring
- 1 small jar of rose petal jelly (or any red fruit jelly)

FOR THE ROSE BUTTER CREAM:

- 500g / 1lb 2oz cups icing sugar * (3½ cups)
- 250g / 9oz soft butter (1 stick + 2 Tbsp)
- 5ml / 1 tsp rose water
- A few drops of natural pink colouring
- A little milk if required

TO DECORATE:

- Approximately 50 white chocolate sticks or scrolls

* Refer to glossary

Method

Serves 10 – 12

1. Make the frosted rose petals the day before you make the cake: Holding one petal at a time, paint both sides with egg white and then sprinkle caster sugar over it. Using tweezers gently shake off the excess sugar. Dry on a wire rack or on a sheet of baking parchment – leave for 24 hours to dry.

2. If you don't have time to frost the petals you can use them 'au-naturel', as I have for this photograph, or you can buy commercially made ones.

3. For the cake: Preheat the oven to 180ºC / 350ºF.

4. Butter the two cake tins and line the base of each with a circle of non-stick baking parchment.

5. Beat the butter and sugar together until pale and fluffy.

6. Add the egg yolks and mix well.

7. Sift the flour and baking powder over the cake mixture. Fold in as lightly as possible, using a large metal spoon.

8. Fold in the ground almonds, the almond essence and the pink colouring – enough to give a delicate rose pink shade to the cake.

Continued ➢

Method Continued

9. Whisk the egg whites until they stand in soft peaks.

10. Fold them into the cake mixture carefully in 3 batches.

11. Divide the mixture between the tins and spread it evenly with a slight hollow in the centre.

12. Bake for 15 – 20 minutes, when cooked it will feel springy to the touch.

13. Leave to cool in the tins for a few minutes before removing and placing on a wire rack to cool completely.

14. While the cake is cooking, make the butter cream: Sift the icing sugar into a bowl and add the butter. Beat with a hand mixer for a couple of minutes. Add the rose water, pink colouring and just as much of the milk as you need to achieve a creamy spreadable texture.

15. To assemble the cake: Spread one of the cake layers with butter cream and one with rose-petal jelly and sandwich together. Spread the top with butter cream. Take a third cake layer and spread with rose-petal jelly and place on top with the jelly-side down. Spread the top with butter cream. Repeat with the fourth layer, finishing with a topping of butter cream.

16. Spread the remaining butter cream around the sides of the cake, taking care to finish it neatly.

17. Position the white chocolate sticks all around the outside of the cake.

18. Just before serving, sprinkle with the rose petals and position birthday candles if required.

19. Store in an airtight container for up to 3 days – although the rose petals won't last this long.

Variation

- I sometimes fill the cake with fresh raspberries, cream and rose petal jelly or raspberry jam instead of butter cream.

A special birthday card that I received from HRH The Princess of Wales and a very young Prince Harry

"I love the challenge of making a special birthday cake ... Two young princes always managed to come up with ideas for their birthday cakes that pushed the art of constructing something out of cake to the limit!"

Sticky Fruit Loaf

This sticky fruit loaf travelled around the world with me on many official royal state visits. It travels well and because it is so moist, it improves with age. Whether we were in a palace or on a train, a boat or a 'plane, it was always a welcome accompaniment to a cup of tea, or the perfect treat to pop into a packed lunch. It is worth shopping around for dried fruit that is extra plump and juicy — I like to use jumbo flame raisins and Orange River sultanas, of South African origin. You can also substitute chopped dried apricots and figs for the raisins and sultanas.

Ingredients

YOU WILL NEED:

A 450g / 1lb loaf tin, approximately 16 x 11cm, 7cm deep (6¼ x 4¼ inches, 2¾ inches deep)

FOR THE CAKE:

- 170g / 6oz soft butter (1½ sticks)
- 170g / 6oz dark soft brown sugar * (¾ cup)
- 3 free-range eggs (UK medium / USA large) *
- 210g / 7½oz plain flour * (1¾ cups)
- 12.5ml / 2½ tsp baking powder
- 10ml / 2 tsp mixed spice *
- 115g / 4oz glacé cherries *
- 115g / 4oz soft plump sultanas (⅔ cup)
- 115g / 4oz soft plump raisins (⅔ cup)

FOR THE SUGAR SYRUP:

- 120ml / ½ cup water
- 55g / 2oz granulated sugar (¼ cup)
- 5ml / 1 tsp pure vanilla extract *
- 1 cinnamon stick

* Refer to glossary

Chef on tour!

Method

Makes one loaf, about 12 slices

1. Preheat the oven to 160ºC / 325ºF.

2. Line the base and sides of the loaf tin with baking parchment.

3. Cream together the butter and sugar until light and fluffy.

4. Beat in the eggs one at a time, adding in 2 tablespoons of flour with the last egg. Sift in the remaining flour and baking powder and spice and mix well.

5. Wash and dry the glacé cherries, cut them in half and dust them lightly with flour (to prevent them from sinking to the bottom of the cake). Lastly mix in all the fruit.

6. Pour into the prepared loaf tin and bake for 50 – 60 minutes.

7. While the cake is baking, make the syrup: Combine all the ingredients in a small heavy-based saucepan, stir while heating to dissolve the sugar and then simmer for 4 minutes. Leave the cinnamon stick in until you use the syrup.

8. While the cake is still warm, glaze it all over with the sugar syrup.

9. After about 30 minutes, remove the cake from the tin and leave to cool on a wire rack.

10. Store in an air-tight container for up to two weeks.

Bountiful Breads

LARGE AND SMALL,
SAVOURY AND SWEET,
COLLECTED FROM FAR AND WIDE

Banana Nut Bread

The best banana bread is made from squidgy bananas; those that some would consider to be over-ripe or certainly too ripe to enjoy eating. Their flavour is at its most robust when they reach this stage. If I only have one or two like this, then I freeze them (in their skins) until I have accumulated enough to make a loaf. When you are ready to make your banana bread, peel them while still frozen and they will quite quickly soften enough for you to mash them. Coconut milk imparts a delicious flavour to the banana bread but you can also use buttermilk or ordinary milk.

Ingredients

YOU WILL NEED:

Twelve mini loaf tins, approximately 7cm x 4cm (2¾ x 1½ inches) OR one large 900g / 2lb loaf tin, approximately 23 x 13cm, 7cm deep (9 x 5 inches, 2¾ inches deep)

- 170g / 6oz soft butter (1½ sticks) + a little extra butter for the sides of the loaf tin
- 170g / 6oz golden caster sugar *
- 115g / 4oz soft light brown sugar *
- 3 free-range eggs, lightly beaten (UK medium / USA large) *
- 350g / 12½oz bananas, roughly mashed
- 85g / 3oz pecans, chopped
- 250g / 9oz plain flour * (2 cups)
- Pinch of salt
- 7.5ml / 1½ tsp bicarbonate of soda *
- 60ml / 4 Tbsp coconut milk
- 5ml / 1 tsp vanilla extract *
- A few banana chips
- A handful of slivered pecans

* Refer to glossary

Method

Makes 12 mini loaves or 1 large loaf

1. Preheat the oven to 170ºC / 325ºF.

2. Line the base of the loaf tins with baking parchment and butter the sides thoroughly.

3. Cream the butter and sugars together by hand or using an electric hand mixer, until the mixture is light and creamy.

4. Add the beaten eggs and 2 tablespoons of the flour, mix well.

5. Mix in the mashed banana and chopped pecans.

6. Sift in the remaining flour, salt and bicarbonate of soda. Fold them into the mixture carefully using a large metal spoon. (Over-mixing at this stage will result in a tough texture.)

7. Lastly mix in the coconut milk and vanilla extract.

8. Spoon the mixture into the loaf tin(s), level it with a small palette knife or spatula and top with a few banana chips and slivered pecans.

9. Place the small loaf tins onto a baking tray and bake for 20 – 25 minutes. Bake the large loaf for 40 – 50 minutes.

10. Leave loaves in their tins for 10 – 15 minutes before removing, then cool thoroughly on a wire rack.

11. Store in an airtight container. The banana bread will keep for a week. It gets better with age; after 2 – 3 days it will be moister than on the day it is baked.

12. Serve either plain or with butter and honey or cream cheese.

Breakfast Muffins

T his is an amazing recipe; you can keep the basic mixture in the fridge for up to 3 weeks. This means that you can bake off just a few muffins at a time and enjoy them freshly made at a moment's notice. There is no warmer welcome for a visitor, than a good cup of coffee and something freshly baked. I use figs but you can substitute any dried fruit or vine fruit.

Note that the mixture should be left overnight before using it. This allows the oat bran to swell, which gives the muffins their silky texture; otherwise the bran can be a little gritty.

Ingredients

YOU WILL NEED:

Two medium / large muffin tins

- 2 free-range eggs (UK medium / USA large) *
- 285g / 10oz demerara or light soft brown sugar * (1⅓ cups)
- 80ml / ⅓ cup oil
- 70g / 2½oz oatbran (¾ cup)
- 450ml / 1¾ cups milk
- 5ml / 1 tsp vanilla extract *
- 5ml / 1 tsp salt
- 285g / 10oz plain flour * (2⅓ cups)
- 15ml / 1 Tbsp bicarbonate of soda *
- 10ml / 2 tsp mixed spice *
- 3oz / 85g soft, plump dried figs, finely sliced (½ cup well packed)

FOR THE TOPPING:

- Use a combination of some or all of the following: 100ml / ½ cup mixed linseeds, poppy seeds, sunflower seeds, sesame seeds, flaked almonds, slivered pecans, chopped pistachios, pumpkin seeds and dried cranberries.

* Refer to glossary

Method

Makes 24 medium or 15 large muffins

1. In a large bowl, beat together the eggs and sugar and then add the oil and mix well.

2. Add all the remaining ingredients, sieving the flour, salt and bicarbonate of soda. Mix well.

3. Cover and leave in the refrigerator overnight to allow the bran to swell.

4. Line the muffin tins with paper cases or 'tulips' of baking parchment.

5. Spoon in the mixture and sprinkle with seeds.

6. Bake at 160ºC / 310ºF for 20 – 25 minutes for medium muffins or, for the large ones, allow 30 – 35 minutes.

7. They are delicious straight from the oven but they do keep for 2 days.

8. Serve with butter, cream cheese, honey, jam, peanut butter or almond butter.

Cinnamon Rolls

W hen I visited Sri Lanka with HRH The Prince of Wales, I bought the most amazing cinnamon in a local market. On my return home, I was so inspired by its wonderfully vibrant flavour and evocative aroma; unlike any cinnamon that I had ever found in a supermarket. I experimented endlessly with ways to use it. Sadly my Sri Lankan bounty ran out long ago, but these rolls will always remind me of that incredible market.

In this recipe I have included some custard powder in the dough, which gives it a really rounded, creamy colour and flavour. The dark muscovado sugar in the filling introduces rich undertones of treacle, while the frosting — made with a splash of fresh lime juice — is beautifully tangy.

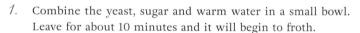
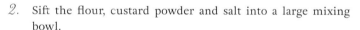

Ingredients

YOU WILL NEED:

One 22cm (8½ inch) square cake tin

FOR THE DOUGH:

- 15ml / 3 tsp dried yeast * (⅓oz)
- 5ml / 1 tsp caster sugar *
- 60ml / 4 Tbsp warm water
- 500g / 1lb 2oz plain flour * (4 cups)
- 35g / 1oz custard powder *
- Pinch of salt
- 1 free-range egg (UK medium / USA large) *
- 225ml / 1 cup milk
- 5ml / 1 tsp vanilla extract *
- 60g / 2oz butter (4 Tbsp)

FOR THE FILLING:

- 60g / 2oz pecans (½ cup)
- 30g / 1oz flaked almonds * (¼ cup)
- 170g / 6oz dark muscovado sugar * (¾ cup)
- 15ml / 3 tsp cinnamon
- 60g / 2oz butter (4 Tbsp)

FOR THE FROSTING:

- 30g / 1oz soft butter (2 Tbsp)
- 115g / 4oz icing sugar * (1 cup)
- 15ml / 3 tsp freshly pressed lime juice

* Refer to glossary

Method

Makes 12

1. Combine the yeast, sugar and warm water in a small bowl. Leave for about 10 minutes and it will begin to froth.

2. Sift the flour, custard powder and salt into a large mixing bowl.

3. Lightly beat the egg, gently warm the milk (it should be tepid) and melt the butter then combine these three ingredients and add the vanilla extract.

4. Make a well in the centre of the dry ingredients and pour in the yeast and most of the milk mixture. Mix to form a smooth, not sticky, dough. Add the remaining liquid if required.

5. Turn it out onto a lightly floured surface and knead the dough for about 10 minutes until it is elastic. When you press your finger into the dough, it should pop out again.

6. Rub the inside of the mixing bowl with butter and return the dough to the bowl. Cover with a clean cloth and leave somewhere warm to rise — (an airing cupboard, the top of an Aga or a sunny windowsill).

7. It will take 45 minutes to an hour for the dough to double in size.

8. While the dough is rising, make the filling: Lightly toast the pecans and almonds and then roughly chop them. Combine them with the sugar, cinnamon and butter. Mix well and keep on one side.

Continued ⇀

Method Continued

9. To make the frosting: Cream the butter with the sifted icing sugar and gradually mix in the lime juice. If it curdles, add a little more icing sugar and chill it in the refrigerator.

10. When the dough has doubled in size, knock it back* on a floured surface and roll it out to a rectangle measuring about 30cm x 40cm (12 x 16 inches).

11. Spread the nut filling all over the dough and roll it up, quite tightly, along the long side, like a Swiss roll.

12. Trim off each end of the roll and cut the remainder into 12 slices each approximately 2.5cm (1 inch) thick.

13. Line the square tin with baking parchment and fit the rolls neatly into the tin in a 3 x 4 configuration.

14. If you are preparing these in the evening ready for breakfast the following morning, you can proceed to this point and then cover the rolls with cling film* and refrigerate overnight.

15. Before baking, bring them to room temperature then leave to rise for about 30 minutes. They will almost double in size again.

16. Preheat the oven to 180ºC / 350ºF.

17. Bake the cinnamon rolls for 18 – 25 minutes. They will turn a lovely golden colour.

18. When they come out of the oven, leave for 10 minutes to cool, before spreading the lime frosting onto them.

19. Eat while fresh and warm.

HIGHGROVE HOUSE

A very kind note that I received from HRH The Prince of Wales on returning from an overseas tour

"When I visited Sri Lanka with HRH The Prince of Wales, I bought the most amazing cinnamon in a local market … I was so inspired by its wonderfully vibrant flavour and evocative aroma … I experimented endlessly with ways to use it."

FLOUR

Flowerpot
CORN BREAD

This is where my South African heritage comes to the fore. I have always loved the delicate, sweet taste of corn (or 'mealies' as they are known in South Africa). Made with puréed corn, mealie bread – which, traditionally, is steamed – has a very soft, dense, almost pudding-like texture. Baking the bread in individual flowerpots as I do in this recipe, results in a much lighter texture but with the same sweet, evocative flavour. For a tempting brunch dish, serve these little breads straight from the oven with crispy bacon, tomatoes and avocado.

Ingredients

YOU WILL NEED:

10 small clay flowerpots:
- Height 6cm (2½ inches)
- Diameter at the bottom 4cm (1½ inches)
- Diameter at the top 6cm (2½ inches)

- 450g / 1lb tinned * or frozen sweet corn
- 55g / 2oz butter (½ stick) plus a little extra for the flower pots
- 30g / 1oz golden caster sugar * (⅛ cup)
- 2 free-range eggs (UK medium / USA large) *
- 150g / 4½oz plain flour * (⅛ cup) plus a little extra for dusting the flowerpots
- 15ml / 1 Tbsp baking powder
- 4ml / ¾ tsp salt
- A pinch of chilli powder
- 5ml / 1 tsp finely chopped parsley

* Refer to glossary

Method

Makes 10 small breads

1. Preheat the oven to 200ºC / 400ºF.

2. Butter the flower pots and dust them with flour. Fit a circle of baking parchment in the base of each one.

3. If using frozen sweet corn, cook it in boiling salted water until tender, drain it and leave to cool. If using tinned sweet corn drain it thoroughly.

4. Blend the sweet corn to a purée using either a stick blender or a liquidiser.

5. Cream the butter and sugar and add the eggs.

6. Mix in the sweet corn purée.

7. Sift in the dry ingredients, add the parsley and mix thoroughly.

8. Spoon the mixture into the flower pots and stand them on a baking tray.

9. Bake for 25 – 30 minutes, until golden on the top. When you test them with a skewer, it should come out clean.

10. These are best eaten on the day they are made, but you can freeze them and reheat them in the oven.

I discovered this bread when I was a student working in a hotel in Mürren, a beautiful ski resort in the Swiss Alps. It is a traditional bread with a very soft crumb and silky texture. For a Swiss-style breakfast serve it with a selection of gorgeous Swiss cheeses and cold meats. I also use this recipe for making a beautiful bunny-shaped Easter bread. This is a brilliant way to spend a few hours when you have tiny, enthusiastic helpers rolling up their sleeves and getting their hands in the dough!

Swiss-Style
BUTTER BREAD

Ingredients

YOU WILL NEED:

Two large flat baking trays at least
25 x 35cm (10 x 14 inches)

- 5ml / 1 tsp quick dried yeast *
- 10ml / 2 tsp caster sugar *
- 500g / 1lb 2oz bread flour * (4 cups)
- 7ml / 1½ tsp salt
- 350ml / 1½ cups milk
- 75g / 2½oz soft butter (5 Tbsp)
- free-range 1 egg (UK medium / USA large) *

* Refer to glossary

Method

Makes 2 large loaves

1. Mix the yeast and sugar in a small bowl and add 15ml (1 tablespoon) of warm water. Leave for 10 minutes until the yeast begins to foam.

2. Sift the flour and salt into a large mixing bowl (or the bowl of a heavy duty mixer).

3. Warm the milk gently and then add most of it to the flour with the yeast and butter.

4. Mix thoroughly to a soft but not sticky dough. Add more milk or flour as required to get the right consistency.

5. Knead the dough for 4 or 5 minutes if using a mixer, or for 10 minutes by hand. If you are making the bread by hand, once the dough is mixed, you can take it out of the bowl and knead it on a lightly floured surface. When it is ready it will be smooth, silky and elastic and when you push your finger into it, it should spring out again.

6. Place the dough into an oiled bowl, cover with a damp tea towel and leave to rise in a warm place. It should double in size, which will take about an hour.

7. Knock the dough back* and knead it again for a few minutes. Divide it in half and then divide each piece into three.

8. Roll each piece into a 'sausage' about 30cm (12 inches) long and then lay them out next to each other. Pinch the strands together at one end, then plait by bringing the left strand over the middle strand, then bring the right strand over the middle strand. Continue like this, alternating bringing the left and right strands into the centre until you reach the end of the dough. Finish by tucking the ends underneath neatly and 'sticking' them down with water.

9. Place the bread onto a baking tray and leave to rise again for about 30 minutes. Preheat the oven to 200ºC / 400ºF.

10. Beat the egg with a little salt and glaze the bread evenly all over. Bake in the centre of the oven for 35 – 40 minutes. Tap the bottom of the loaf and it will sound hollow when it is cooked.

11. For a soft crust, wrap the bread in a damp tea towel as soon as it comes out of the oven. For a crisp crust, leave to cool on a wire rack.

12. This bread is at its best fresh from the oven, but will keep for a couple of days if wrapped. It also makes lovely toast.

Thyme Focaccia
WITH GOATS' CHEESE AND POTATO

During my time as a royal chef, HRH The Prince of Wales sent me to Italy where I worked in several restaurant kitchens and had the privilege of learning from some of the very best Italian chefs. I particularly enjoyed making local speciality breads. You can vary the toppings on this focaccia: tomatoes, roasted peppers, caramelised shallots and red onions are all wonderful. Sometimes I just slip extra goats' cheese onto this bread and eat it fresh from the oven - bread and cheese doesn't get any better than this!

Ingredients

YOU WILL NEED:

Two flat baking trays

- 500g / 1lb 2oz bread flour * (4 cups)
- 10 ml / 2 tsp easy blend yeast *
- 10 ml / 2 tsp salt
- 6 large sprigs of thyme
- 60ml / 4 Tbsp extra virgin olive oil
- 60g / 2oz pine nuts, * toasted (½ cup)
- 300ml / 1¼ cup tepid water
- 170g / 6oz goats' cheese
- 300g / 10½oz cooked waxy new potatoes *
- 10ml / 2 tsp salt flakes
- Freshly ground black pepper
- 75ml / ⅓ cup lemon oil (or finely grate the zest of 1 lemon into 75ml / ⅓ cup olive oil)

* Refer to glossary

Method

Makes 2 rounds of bread, approximately 24cm (9½ inches) in diameter

1. Sift the flour, yeast and salt into a large mixing bowl.

2. Add the thyme leaves from 3 of the stems, the olive oil, pine nuts and most of the water. Stir until a rough dough forms.

3. Using your hands, bring the dough together, turn it out onto a floured surface and knead for 10 minutes or until it is very smooth and 'elastic'.

4. Return to the large bowl, which has been greased with a little olive oil. Cover with a clean, damp cloth and leave in a warm place to rise, until it has doubled in size. This will take about an hour.

5. Knock back the dough* and divide it into two. Shape into 2 round, flat loaves about 20cm (8 inches) in diameter and place them each onto an oiled baking sheet.

6. Cover loosely with oiled cling film* and leave in a warm place to rise again; this time for about 20 minutes. Preheat the oven to 190ºC / 375ºF.

7. When risen, make holes in the top of each loaf using your finger.

8. Slice the potatoes and goats' cheese thinly and toss onto the 2 loaves. Decorate with the remaining thyme and sprinkle with salt flakes and freshly ground black pepper. Drizzle with half of the lemon oil.

9. Bake for 40 – 50 minutes until the bread is well risen and golden and sounds hollow when you tap it on the bottom.

10. When it comes out of the oven, drizzle with the remaining lemon oil and serve as soon as possible.

11. This bread is ideal for a picnic. Bake it just before you go and wrap it in foil and then in a tea towel and it will stay warm for quite a long time.

Scones

WITH VANILLA AND ORANGE ZEST

O ne of the abiding memories I have of the Garden Parties that I attended at Buckingham Palace, is of the mountains of cream scones and cucumber sandwiches. Forever more, scones will be synonymous with Garden Parties for me. This is my favourite recipe for scones and my advice is to eat them fresh from the oven and never to stint on the cream and jam!

Ingredients

YOU WILL NEED:

A 4cm (1½ inch) pastry cutter and 2 flat baking trays

- 450g / 1lb plain flour * (3¾ cup)
- 60g / 2oz golden caster sugar * (⅓ cup)
- 2.5ml / ½ tsp salt
- 15ml / 3 tsp baking powder
- 100g / 3½oz butter (7 Tbsp)
- 175ml / ¾ cup buttermilk
- 50ml / ¼ cup milk
- 1 free-range egg (UK medium / USA large) *
- 5ml / 1 tsp vanilla extract *
- Zest of 1 orange

* Refer to glossary

The Lord Chamberlain is commanded by Her Majesty to invite

Miss Carolyn Robb

to a Garden Party at Buckingham Palace on Wednesday 21st July 1999 from 4 to 6 pm

This card does not admit

I remember this garden party well as it poured with rain, resulting in a lot of very droopy hats!

Method

Makes approximately 15 scones

1. Preheat the oven to 220ºC / 425ºF.

2. Sieve the flour, sugar, salt and baking powder into a large mixing bowl.

3. Rub the butter into the dry ingredients using your finger tips, until the mixture resembles breadcrumbs.

4. Blend together the buttermilk, milk, egg and vanilla extract.

5. Make a hollow in the centre of the 'crumbs', finely grate the orange zest into it and pour in most of the liquid. Add in the remainder later if the dough seems dry. Traditionally, a small round-bladed knife or palette knife is used to mix the dough. You want to achieve a lightly-bound dough that is neither sticky nor dry and crumbly.

6. Lift the ball of dough onto a floured surface and knead it just 3 or 4 times to get rid of any cracks, working quickly. If the dough is over-worked it will result in 'tough' scones.

7. Pat the dough out to a thickness of 2cm (¾ inch). Cut out the scones, dipping the pastry cutter into flour each time, so that it makes a clean cut and does not drag the dough when cutting through it. Place scones onto the baking trays.

8. Gather the trimmings, lightly bring them together and pat the dough out again to cut out more scones.

9. Bake for 10 – 12 minutes, until well risen and golden.

10. For fruit scones, add in 60g (⅓ cup) sultanas or raisins at Step 5. For savoury scones, replace the vanilla, orange zest and sugar with 60g (½ cup) of grated mature cheddar cheese and 15ml (1 tablespoon) finely chopped chives, added in at Step 5; top with a little extra cheese and a light dusting of paprika.

FLOUR

Soda Bread

O f all the breads in this chapter, this is my favourite. It is simple, wholesome and quick to make. Be careful not to over-mix the dough. Unlike other breads, which require kneading to make them lighter, this dough requires as little handling as possible for a light texture. Don't be alarmed if, a few hours after baking, you notice that any of the pine nuts or sunflower seeds in the bread have turned bright green. This is caused by a reaction between the anti-oxidants in the seeds and the bicarbonate of soda and it is nothing to worry about.

Ingredients

YOU WILL NEED:

One flat baking sheet, at least 23cm (9 inches) wide

- 225g / 8oz plain flour * (2 cups)
- 10ml / 2 tsp bicarbonate of soda *
- 5ml / 1 tsp salt
- 225g / 8oz malted granary or whole wheat flour * (2 cups)
- 30g / 1oz soft butter (2 Tbsp) and a little extra butter for greasing the baking sheet
- 375ml / 1½ cups milk
- 125ml / ½ cup plain yoghurt
- 30ml / 2 Tbsp barley malt extract *
- 15ml / 1 Tbsp sesame seeds
- 15ml / 1 Tbsp linseed *

* Refer to glossary

Variations

1. Add a handful of chopped fresh herbs of your choice: parsley, chives, thyme, rosemary and sage all work well.

2. For a sweet bread, add a handful of chopped plump dried figs or dates and a few pecans. Sprinkle the top with a little cinnamon sugar instead of seeds.

Method

Makes 1 round loaf, approximately 23cm (9 inches) in diameter

1. Preheat the oven to 200ºC / 400ºF.

2. Rub a little butter onto the baking sheet.

3. Sift the flour, bicarbonate of soda and salt into the largest mixing bowl that you have, tip in any whole grains that don't go through the sieve.

4. Rub the butter into the dry ingredients, using your fingertips.

5. Whisk together the milk, yoghurt and malt extract. Make a well in the centre of the dry ingredients and pour in most of the milk mixture; reserving a little to add in later if needed.

6. Working as quickly and lightly as possible with a round-bladed knife, mix the dough and then bring it together into one ball with your hands; it will be soft and still slightly sticky. Tip it onto a lightly floured surface and, without kneading it, shape it into a round of about 20cm (8 inches) in diameter and about 3 – 4cm (1¼ – 1½ inches) thick. The less the dough is handled, the lighter the bread will be.

7. Lift the bread onto the baking sheet, re-shaping if necessary. Cut a deep cross in the top and sprinkle with seeds.

8. Bake for 30 – 40 minutes until the bread is golden. To check if it is cooked, tap it on the bottom – it will sound hollow when ready. Cool on a wire rack.

9. For a crisp crust, leave the bread uncovered. For a soft crust, rub a little butter onto the crust as soon as the bread comes out of the oven then wrap the bread in some baking parchment paper and then in a slightly damp tea-towel.

10. This is best served very fresh from the oven, while it is still warm. Traditionally, it is broken into quarters and then sliced. It also makes very good toast on day two!

FLOUR

Quick-Mix
CHEESE AND TOMATO BREAD

For a quick lunch of bread and cheese, you can throw this loaf together in a matter of minutes. Serve it with good farmhouse butter, a hunk of mature cheddar cheese and some home-made chutney (see recipe on page 249). It is also scrumptious for a picnic; bake it just before you leave and wrap it in foil and a tea towel to keep it warm.

Ingredients

YOU WILL NEED:

A 450g / 1lb loaf tin, approximately 16 x 11cm, 7cm deep (6¼ x 4¼ inches, 2¾ inches deep)

- 285g / 10oz plain flour * (2⅓ cups)
- 15ml / 1 Tbsp baking powder
- A generous pinch of salt
- 85g / 3oz butter (6 Tbsp)
- 130g / 4½oz extra mature cheddar cheese, grated (1 cup)
- 15ml / 1 Tbsp finely chopped parsley
- 15ml / 1 Tbsp finely chopped chives
- ½ red onion
- 4 sundried tomatoes (approx 30g / 1oz)
- 1 free-range egg (UK medium / USA large) *
- 125ml (½ cup) milk
- 15g / ½oz butter (1 Tbsp)
- 15ml / 1 Tbsp finely chopped parsley to sprinkle on top

* Refer to glossary

Method

Makes 1 medium loaf, serves 4 – 6

1. Preheat the oven to 200ºC / 400ºF.

2. Line the base of the loaf tin with baking parchment and grease the sides with butter.

3. Sift the flour, baking powder and salt into a large mixing bowl. Rub in the butter.

4. Mix in ¾ of the grated cheese into the dry ingredients with the herbs.

5. Finely chop the onion and dice the sundried tomatoes, add to the dry ingredients.

6. Whisk the egg and milk together and add to the dry ingredients.

7. Mix carefully. All the flour should be mixed in, but do not over-mix or you will have tough bread.

8. Spoon mixture into the prepared loaf tin.

9. Melt the butter and drizzle it over the loaf. Sprinkle with the remaining grated cheese and parsley.

10. Bake for 30 – 40 minutes until golden. Check if the loaf is cooked by inserting a skewer; it will come out clean if the loaf is ready.

11. This bread is best eaten on the day that it is made, but the next day it makes wonderful toast.

12. It makes lovely individual loaves if baked in mini loaf tins for 18 – 20 minutes.

Warm
HERB BREAD

Herb bread is a refreshing alternative to garlic bread and you don't need to worry about breathing garlic over anyone after eating it! The fresh herbs and lemon give off a wonderfully enticing aroma while it is baking. You can vary the herbs according to seasonal availability, what might be growing in your garden and personal preference.

Ingredients

- 1 white baguette
- 1 granary or multi-grain baguette

FOR THE HERB BUTTER:
- A handful each of fresh parsley, thyme, chives and basil
- 150g / 5½oz butter
- 4 stems of fresh thyme
- Zest and juice of 1 lemon
- Salt and freshly ground black pepper

Method

Makes 2 loaves, serves 6 – 8

1. Make the herb butter: Remove the thyme leaves from the stems. Chop all of the remaining herbs and add them to the thyme.

2. Cream the butter until soft, mix in the herbs, grate in the lemon zest and add the lemon juice. Season to taste with salt and pepper.

3. Heat the oven to 200ºC / 400ºF.

4. Slice the loaves and butter each slice on both sides.

5. Reassemble each loaf on a sheet of aluminium foil, alternating the slices of white and granary bread.

6. Spread some more herb butter along the top and lay two springs of thyme on each loaf.

7. Wrap the bread in the foil, place on a baking tray.

8. Bake for 15 minutes then open the foil and bake for a further 10 minutes to crisp the top. Serve immediately.

Serving Suggestion

1. This is an excellent accompaniment to any pasta dish.

2. For a simple appetiser, serve with kalamata olive tapenade.

3. For a quick lunch, serve with an oven-baked Camembert and a green salad.

Tracklements & Treats
FROM THE PRESERVING PAN

Apple Butter

Making apple butter is a great way to preserve apples when they are in abundance. It is a highly concentrated form of apple sauce, which is cooked long and slow, allowing the sugar to caramelise and the liquid to evaporate, resulting in a firm apple 'paste'. The apples require no peeling or coring – just wash and roughly chop them. I like to add some vanilla extract and orange zest at the end of the cooking process, it makes the apple butter delightfully aromatic. I use half Bramley cooking apples and half Coxes English Pippin eating apples, but you can use any apples for this recipe.

When I find myself preparing a large quantity of apples, it always brings back happy and fond memories of a bitterly cold and wet Autumn day spent pressing apples in the stable yard at Highgrove. We had many crates overflowing with apples and a traditional old wooden cider press, which had been borrowed from an apple farmer in Somerset (the heart of 'cider country'). Wearing 'wellies and waterproofs' in place of our usual pristine white chefs' jackets and aprons, we made gallons of the most delicious apple juice and had enormous fun in the process. It was one of those days when I remember thinking 'I have the best job in the world'... and I did!

Ingredients

YOU WILL NEED:
Two 450g / 1lb jam jars or Kilner preserving jars

- 1kg / 2lbs 4oz apples
- 250ml / 1 cup water
- 250g / 9oz soft brown sugar * (1 cup)
- 5ml / 1 tsp pure vanilla extract *
- Zest of 1 orange

* Refer to glossary

Method

Makes approximately 1kg / 2lbs, depending on how much the apple butter reduces.

1. Wash and dry the apples but do not peel them.

2. Cut them into medium-sized pieces, including the cores.

3. Place them in a heavy-based pan with the water.

4. Bring to the boil and then reduce the heat and simmer with the lid on for 20 – 30 minutes, until the fruit is very soft. The variety of apples used will determine how long it takes for the fruit to soften.

5. Rub the fruit through a sieve into a large bowl or put it through a vegetable mill.

6. Return the pulp to the cleaned pan with the sugar, stir to mix in the sugar and simmer it gently over a very low heat for at least an hour, stirring frequently. It bubbles up and splatters everywhere, so be careful that you don't get burnt hands and keep a close eye on it as it burns easily.

7. The volume of apple will reduce by about one third and it will gradually thicken.

Continued ⇢

Method Continued

8. When the apple butter is ready, it will be very thick and will have a 'creamy' texture.

9. Lastly, add the vanilla extract and the orange zest and stir well.

10. Fill pre-warmed and sterilised jars with the apple butter.

11. Leave to cool completely before sealing.

12. When the apple butter is cold it will be firm enough to cut.

13. Store in the refrigerator for up to six weeks.

Variations

- Add 15ml / 1 Tbsp of finely chopped crystallised ginger to the apple pulp when you add the sugar.

- For delicately spiced apple butter, add 2.5ml / ½ tsp each of ground nutmeg, cinnamon and cloves to the apple pulp when you add the sugar.

- Instead of cooking the apples in water, use 250ml / 1 cup medium sweet cider. This makes the apple butter a little more acidic.

Serving Suggestions

1. Spread it on toast, chunky farmhouse bread or scones.

2. Serve on a cheese board, as you would Quince cheese (Dulce de Membrillo).

3. Use as a cake filling. To make it soft and spreadable, you may need to warm it a little and beat it with a wooden spoon.

4. Spoon a little onto discs of puff pastry, fold in half and crimp together to make little apple turnovers.

5. For a delicious apple pie, spread some apple butter into the base of a pie crust and top with sautéed apple slices, sprinkle with cinnamon sugar and bake.

6. Serve it with pork, instead of traditional apple sauce.

7. Add a little to a sausage casserole for a lovely hint of apple.

Wishing you a very Happy Christmas
and New Year

A Christmas Card from
HRH The Prince of Wales

"When I find myself preparing a large quantity of apples, it always brings back happy and fond memories of a bitterly cold and wet Autumn day spent pressing apples in the stable yard at Highgrove."

Butterscotch Sauce

I love the word 'Butterscotch' almost as much as I love the real thing! It evokes wonderful sweet, indulgent childhood culinary memories. The characteristic buttery caramel flavour is created by cooking butter and brown sugar together. There are numerous recipes for butterscotch sauce, but this is undoubtedly the ultimate one. I use honey, malt extract and orange zest, which together give it a lovely depth of flavour, whilst the cream and vanilla in it, make it rich and smooth, without the sauce being over-sweet.

Ingredients

- 60g / 2oz butter (4 Tbsp)
- 115g / 4oz light soft brown sugar * or light muscovado sugar * (½ cup)
- 60ml / 4 Tbsp honey
- 15ml / 1 Tbsp barley malt extract *
- 225ml / 1 cup double cream *
- Zest of 1 orange
- 5ml / 1 tsp pure vanilla extract *

* Refer to glossary

Method

Makes 300ml / 1⅓ cups

1. In a small heavy-based pan melt the butter with the sugar.

2. Cook together for 2 – 3 minutes, allowing it to bubble gently.

3. Add the honey, malt extract and cream. Bring to a gentle simmer and cook for a further minute or two.

4. Remove from the heat. Grate the orange zest very finely, directly into the sauce and add the vanilla extract.

5. Mix well.

6. When cool, store in a sealed glass jar in the refrigerator for up to 2 weeks.

Serving Suggestions

1. It is the ultimate Sticky Toffee Pudding sauce.

2. Drizzle over vanilla or coffee ice cream and add sliced banana and toasted almonds for a sophisticated Banana Split.

3. Perfect for waffles or crêpes.

4. Spoon over baked apples.

5. For a hearty winter pudding, serve with a slice of warm ginger cake (see recipe on page 182)

Dried-Apricot Jam
WITH VANILLA

Apricots and vanilla are heavenly together. I leave the vanilla pods in this jam when it is bottled, which allows the flavour to develop further with time. Using dried apricots means you don't have to wait for them to be in season and the jam has a deliciously intense apricot flavour. The colour of the jam will vary according to the apricots that you use. Naturally dried ones, which do have the best flavour, will yield a dark jam. Apricots dried with the addition of sulphites (which preserve their bright colour) will yield a lighter coloured jam, with a soft set.

Ingredients

YOU WILL NEED:
6 x 455g / 1lb glass jars with lids that seal

- 450g / 1lb dried apricots
- 3 vanilla pods
- 1.5 litres / 6¾ cups water
- Juice and zest of 1 lemon
- 1.6kg / 3½ lbs preserving sugar * (7 cups)
- A knob of butter (1 Tbsp)

* Refer to glossary

Serving Suggestions

1. Spread generously onto hot buttered toast; it is especially good on toasted Soda Bread (see recipe on page 220).

2. Perfect for cream scones (see recipe on page 219).

3. Use in biscuits, such as Jam Drops (see recipe on page 166).

4. Delicious as a cake filling in a Victoria Sandwich (see recipe on page 190).

5. For a quick dessert, stir a spoonful into some Greek yoghurt and sprinkle with chopped pistachios or toasted almonds.

Method

Makes approximately 3kg / 6lbs of jam

1. Finely dice the dried apricots and slit the vanilla pods lengthwise and then in half. Place them together in a large bowl with the water, lemon juice and lemon zest.

2. Cover and leave in a cool place to soak for 24 hours.

3. Place in a large heavy-based pan or a preserving pan and bring to the boil. Simmer until the fruit is tender. Depending on the dried fruit used, this will take 20 – 30 minutes.

4. Add the sugar and stir until dissolved.

5. Bring to the boil and keep it on a rolling boil for another 20 – 30 minutes, until setting point is reached.

6. To test if the jam is ready, drop a spoonful onto a small plate and place it in the freezer for about 5 minutes. It should form a 'skin' and when it is ready it will 'wrinkle' when you run your finger through it. Continue cooking and testing until this stage is reached.

7. Leave to stand for a few moments. Then, using a large metal spoon, skim any 'scum' off the top of the jam.

8. Stir in a knob of butter as this will help to disperse any remaining scum, leaving a beautifully clear jam.

9. Pour into pre-warmed, sterilised jars. Put one or two pieces of vanilla pod into each jar.

10. Cool completely before covering the surface of the jam in each jar with a disc of baking parchment or a thin layer of melted wax. Seal with a screw-top lid. Store in a cool, dark place. Keeps for at least 12 months. Refrigerate once opened.

Flavoured Sugars

These are very simple to make and they look wonderful lined up on any larder shelf. There are endless ways to use them and they make lovely gifts. Experiment with your own flavours, using raw sugar as well as the refined varieties. The only rule is to use flavourings that will not introduce moisture into the sugar. In just moments you can make a wonderful gift for any coffee lover: Fill a jar with rough-cut brown and white sugar lumps and toss in a handful of freshly roasted coffee beans. Seal the jar and leave it for about a week. When you open it, the sugar will have absorbed some of that wonderful 'freshly roasted coffee bean' aroma. Used in coffee, this as good as adding another shot, without the extra caffeine!

CHOCOLATE SUGAR

Ingredients

YOU WILL NEED:

Screw-top jam jars or Kilner preserving jars

- 350g / 12½oz granulated sugar (1¾ cups)
- 60g / 2oz good quality dark chocolate chunks (⅓ cup)
- 100g / 3½oz good quality milk chocolate chunks (½ cup)

Method

1. Place all the ingredients in a food processor and blend until the chocolate is broken down into small pieces.

2. Fill your chosen jar with the sugar.

Uses

1. For amazing hot chocolate, heat a generous cup of full cream milk* in a small pan with a heaped teaspoon each of unsweetened cocoa powder and chocolate sugar, a pinch of ground cinnamon and of nutmeg and a few drops of vanilla essence.

2. Use in cake batters, cookie dough and muffin mixes.

GINGER SUGAR

Ingredients

YOU WILL NEED:

Screw-top jam jars or Kilner preserving jars

- 350g / 12½oz soft light brown sugar * (1¾ cups)
- 15ml / 1 Tbsp ground ginger
- 12 pieces of crystallised ginger

* Refer to glossary

Method

1. Combine all the ingredients and fill your chosen jar.

Uses

1. Use in ginger cake (see recipe on page 182) and in ginger biscuits.

2. Sprinkle onto ham before cooking for a delicious glaze.

3. Use to sweeten baked apples.

Flavoured Sugars Continued

VANILLA SUGAR

Ingredients

YOU WILL NEED:

Screw top jam jars or Kilner preserving jars

- 175g / 6oz caster sugar * (¾ cup)
- 175g / 6oz golden caster sugar * (¾ cup)
- 1 large, plump vanilla pod

* Refer to glossary

Method

1. Pour the white and golden sugar into a jar in alternate layers, each one about 1cm / ½ inch deep.

2. Split the vanilla pod in half lengthwise and push it into the sugar.

3. Leave for at least 2 weeks before using the sugar, to allow the flavour to develop.

Uses

1. Adds a wonderful flavour to shortbread, cookies and cakes, such as my Mile-high Mini Victoria Sandwiches (see recipe on page 190).

2. Sprinkle onto strawberries and cream or use in home-made vanilla ice cream (see recipe on page 123).

ORANGE SUGAR

Ingredients

YOU WILL NEED:

Screw top jam jars or Kilner preserving jars

- 350g / 12½oz granulated sugar (1¾ cups)
- 3 oranges

Method

1. Peel the oranges thinly using a vegetable peeler, leaving as little of the bitter white zest on the skin as possible. Place the orange peel onto a rack and dry it out in the oven at 120ºC / 230ºF for 45 – 60 minutes. Keep a close eye on it to be sure that it doesn't colour.

2. When completely dried out, place the peel in a food processor with the sugar and process it. The sugar will become an attractive pale shade of orange. Sieve it to remove any remaining coarse pieces of peel and pour it in your chosen jar. You can keep a whole piece of peel to put in the jar as decoration.

Uses

1. Use in the Marmalade Cake (see recipe on page 185).

2. Stir into hot cocoa or hot chocolate.

3. Sprinkle onto crème brûlée and caramelise.

4. Sprinkle onto crêpes with lemon juice.

Flavoured Sugars Continued

CINNAMON SUGAR

Ingredients

YOU WILL NEED:
Screw top jam jars or Kilner preserving jars

- 350g / 12½oz caster sugar * (1¾ cups)
- 20ml / 4 tsp of ground cinnamon
- 3 cinnamon sticks

* Refer to glossary

Method

1. Sprinkle the ground cinnamon into the sugar and spoon it into the jar in a 'swirled' design.

2. Push the cinnamon sticks into the sugar.

3. Seal and use as desired.

Uses

1. Use for the topping on the Cinnamon Sugar Cake (see recipe on page 189).

2. As a child, I had cinnamon sugar sprinkled onto hot buttered toast for a treat when I got home from school in the winter. Delicious!

3. Sweeten hot chocolate or coffee with it.

4. For a quick dessert, sprinkle peach halves with a little cinnamon sugar, bake until soft and serve with crème fraîche and Amaretti biscuits.

ROSE PETAL SUGAR

Ingredients

YOU WILL NEED:
Screw top jam jars or Kilner preserving jars

- 350g / 12½oz caster sugar * (1¾ cups)
- A handful of dried pink rose petals, either home-dried or from a speciality cake decorating supplier.

* Refer to glossary

Method

1. Place the sugar and petals in a food processor and process until the sugar turns a lovely pink colour and the petals have been completely pulverised.

2. Pass through a medium-fine sieve to remove any remaining coarse pieces of rose petal.

3. Pour into your chosen jar. For presentation purposes you can include a few whole petals in the jar.

Uses

1. Use for decorating fairy cakes, cupcakes or cakes, such as the Rose Petal Cake (see recipe on page 197).

2. Mix into whipped cream and serve with strawberries and raspberries.

This takes me back to my childhood! For my 7th birthday my grandparents gave me a wooden spoon, a mixing bowl and my first cook book (Margaret Powell's book of Sweet Making for Children), all of which I still have and still use. To this day, the wooden spoon is reserved solely for fudge-making.

Fudge

Ingredients

YOU WILL NEED:

One 20cm (8inch) square cake tin, lined with baking parchment

- 1 small tin * sweetened condensed milk (400g / 14oz)
- 400g / 14oz granulated sugar (2 cups)
- 45ml / 3 Tbsp golden syrup *
- 115g / 4oz butter (1 stick)
- 10ml / 2 tsp vinegar
- 5ml / 1 tsp vanilla extract *

* Refer to glossary

Serving Suggestions

1. A beautiful little box of home-made fudge makes a great gift!

2. Serve a square or two with coffee.

3. Crumble over vanilla ice cream.

4. Try crumbling 55g (2oz) of fudge into the Melting Moment dough before shaping the cookies, (see recipe on page 170). Serve either plain or sandwiched together with Dulce de Leche.

Method

Makes approximately 64 pieces each 2cm (1 inch) square

1. Place the condensed milk, sugar, golden syrup and butter in a heavy-based pan. Stir over a low heat, until the sugar dissolves.

2. Bring to the boil and then simmer for 10 – 15 minutes, stirring continuously and scraping the bottom of the pan. (It burns easily if not kept moving).

3. Be extremely careful while cooking and stirring the fudge as it is VERY HOT.

4. To test if the fudge is ready, drop a teaspoonful of the mixture into a bowl of ice-cold water. A soft ball should form. (You can also check using a sugar thermometer; it should be 118°C / 235°F – though I have always successfully used the water method).

5. When ready, remove from the heat and mix in the vinegar and vanilla extract. Beat well for a minute or so and the fudge should start to crystallise on the sides of the saucepan. If it doesn't do this, then return to the stove and simmer for a few more minutes before pouring into the prepared tin.

6. At this stage you can toss in a handful of pecans or raisins or, for delicious chocolate fudge, add 120g / 4oz dark chocolate and beat well, then pour it into the tin.

7. Leave to cool for about 20 minutes, the fudge should not have hardened completely.

8. Using the baking parchment, lift the fudge out of the tin and place on a chopping board. Using a sharp knife with a long blade, cut the fudge into 64 small squares (8 x 8).

9. Leave to cool completely before packing into an airtight container or glass jar. Keeps for 2 weeks; longer than this and it becomes a little dry.

Lemon Curd

W hen I was a child, we had a huge and prolific lemon tree in our garden in South Africa. Lemon curd was something that my mother and I often made together as a way of using up a few lemons. As a teenager, I won quite a few prizes for my lemon curd in the cookery section of the home-crafts at the local agricultural show, where my mother and I competed against one another! Here is my prize-winning recipe.

Ingredients

YOU WILL NEED:
One sterilised 450g / 1lb glass jar with lid, a double boiler *

- 2 free-range eggs (UK medium / USA large) *
- 200g / 7oz caster sugar * (1 cup)
- 140g / 5oz butter
- 2 un-waxed lemons, * zest and juice (Meyer lemons are particularly delicious.)

* Refer to glossary

Method

Makes one 450g / 1lb jar

1. Beat the eggs then put them in the top of a double boiler with the caster sugar, butter, lemon zest and strained lemon juice. Bring the water in the bottom of the double boiler to a gentle simmer. Alternatively, you can use a glass bowl over a saucepan of simmering water. Be careful not to overheat the mixture as it will curdle.

2. Stir well to dissolve the sugar and cook for 15 – 20 minutes until the curd has thickened. (It will thicken further when it cools).

3. Pour into pre-warmed sterilised jar and seal when completely cold.

4. Keeps in the fridge for up to 2 weeks.

Variations

1. For a lovely 'mixed-citrus' curd, add in some lime and orange zest, to taste.

2. Mix in a tablespoon of orange flower water just before bottling, it gives the lemon curd a lovely delicate aroma.

Uses

1. Spread on toast, bread or scones.

2. Mix with an equal quantity of whipped cream and use as a filling for cakes, roulades, profiteroles, meringues and tartlets (see recipe on page 169).

3. For a quick dessert, spoon over ice cream or mix into natural yoghurt and serve with fresh berries.

Orange, Lemon
& LIME CORDIAL

Home-made cordial is very simple to make and is so much healthier than any of the commercially produced cordials. In this recipe, you can tinker with the proportions of orange, lemon and lime until you find the balance that is perfect for you. We always had this in the refrigerator at home. It was made from our home-grown citrus and we called it 'home-brew'. A variation of this recipe, using only lemons and called 'Lemon Refresher' is enjoyed by many members of the Royal Family.

Ingredients

YOU WILL NEED:

2 glass bottles with stoppers or screw top lids

- 900g / 2lb granulated sugar (4½ cups)
- 850ml / 3½ cups water
- Zest and juice of:
  - 2 large un-waxed oranges *
  - 1 un-waxed lemon
  - 1 un-waxed lime
- 20ml / 4 tsp tartaric acid *

* Refer to glossary

Method

Makes 1.5 litres / 2½ pints concentrated cordial

1. Place the sugar and water into a saucepan and bring it to the boil. Stir well to dissolve the sugar. Boil for 3 – 4 minutes.

2. Place the citrus into a large bowl with the tartaric acid and pour the hot sugar syrup onto it.

3. Leave to infuse overnight.

4. Add the citrus juice and then strain and bottle the cordial.

5. Leave to cool completely before sealing the bottles.

6. Store in the refrigerator for up to 4 weeks.

7. To serve, dilute with 4-5 parts of iced water to one part cordial, using either still or carbonated water.

8. For a refreshing summer's drink, mix with carbonated water and plenty of ice, thin slices of cucumber and lime and some mint leaves.

Variations

1. If you add the pulp of 4 passion fruit to the citrus zest before leaving to soak overnight, the flavour is amazing.

2. Mint brings a lovely fresh flavour to the cordial; add a few sprigs and stems to the citrus zest before leaving to soak overnight.

Rich Chocolate Sauce

*F*riends and clients often ask me for copies of my recipes, which I always love to share. This recipe is undoubtedly the one that I have given away more than any other. Served warm, the sauce is smooth, indulgent and is the perfect companion to vanilla ice cream (see recipe on page 123). Eaten cold, by the spoonful, straight from the jar (whilst hiding behind the refrigerator door) it seems to be equally popular!

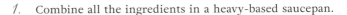

Ingredients

- 120g / 4oz butter (1 stick)
- 120g / 4oz light soft brown sugar * (½ cup)
- 60g / 2oz golden syrup * (3 Tbsp)
- 60g / 2oz good quality dark chocolate (⅓ cup)
- 30ml / 2 Tbsp unsweetened cocoa powder
- 100ml / ⅓ cup double cream *
- 5ml / 1 tsp vanilla extract *

* Refer to glossary

Method

Makes 350ml / ½ pint

1. Combine all the ingredients in a heavy-based saucepan.

2. Heat gently to melt the butter and chocolate and stir to dissolve the sugar.

3. Simmer gently for 1 minute, keep stirring constantly as it catches and burns very easily.

4. Serve immediately or pour into a glass jar to store.

5. Cool completely before sealing the jar. Store in the refrigerator. Keeps for 3 weeks.

Variations

Add 2 tablespoons of a liqueur of your choice:

Crème de Menthe for a choc-mint sauce,

Cointreau for choc-orange sauce,

Amaretto for choc-almond sauce.